"Are They All Yours?"

A documentary of Humanly Unpremeditated Existences

By Irene Georgina Mapother

"Are They All Yours?"

A documentary of Humanly Unpremeditated Existences

By Irene Georgina Mapother

San Antonio, Texas

Are They All Yours?
All Rights Reserved
Copyright © 2015 Irene Mapother
v2.0
Editing by
Cover art designed by

PUBLISHER'S NOTE

The opinions expressed in this manuscript are solely the opinions of the author in addition, do not represent the opinions or thoughts of the Publisher. The author has represented and warranted full ownership and/or legal right to publish all the materials in this book.

The publisher does not have any control over and does not assume any responsibility for author or third party websites or their content.

This book may not be reproduced, transmitted, or stored in whole or in part by any means, including graphic, electronic, or mechanical without the express written consent of the publisher except in the case of brief quotations embodied in critical articles and reviews. Any reproductions without written permission from the publisher is illegal and punishable by law. Please purchase only from authorized distributors to protect the author's rights.

Harrison House Publishing
www.theharrisonhousepublishing.com
info@theharrisonhousepublising.com
ISBN: 978-09861285-2-3
Library of Congress Control Number: 2015943236
Harrison House Publishing and the "HH" logo are trademarks belonging to Harrison House Publishing.

PRINTED IN THE UNITED STATES OF AMERICA

Dedicated to:

My natural husband, my ten connatural children, 17 grandchildren, 10 great grand children, all sweet and brave people who have been my oxygen stabilizers.

Kudos to my granddaughter Serena K. Rodriguez who heroically typed up this manuscript for love.

Dedicated to housewives all over America—no matter "how many ya' got?" (Come to think of it, why does it matter if they are all yours? Or not?)

Dedicated more precisely to:

Lynn Bertis who helped me find faith in words again. She being a professional musician, author of songs, mother of eleven children, wife of an Italian Real Estate Agent, active member of the Roman Catholic church---found spare time to read my words and to give formative comments on them—to laugh in her heartwarming Irish McSharry fashion by stomping the floor with both feet, and letting the laughter roll from the larynx.

"At our first birth we were born of necessity without our knowledge."
– *Four Witnesses by Rod Bennett*

Augustine said: "Neither did my mother make or educate herself. Thou createst her. Nor did her father and mother know what one should come of them."

"Who Made Me?"
"Did not my God Who is not only Goodness but Goodness itself?"
-*St. Augustine's Confessions*

Table of Contents

Introduction: A Must 1

A Short Blunt-Edged Scream 9

PhD's in the Kitchen 19

Why Philosophy? 43

Can You Remember All Their Names? 63

Pardon Our Human Love 81

And Madeline said: 105

The Art of Saying "No" 119

Humanly Unpremeditated Existences 135

"Get a Job!" 145

Ladies - The Basis of Leisure 159

Split Ends 171

A McDonald Catharsis 189

Introduction: A Must

"Words! Words! Words!" "The World *is* full of too many words already! Please don't burden the peoples of the world with any more 'words!'" cajoled my philosopher husband as he sat sandwiched in between the .flowing volumes of the rotund and lovable St. Thomas of Aquinas—flanked in the rear by Heidegger, Jung, Freud, Kant, Adler, Nietzsche, Sarte, Husserll, St. Augustine - - while being mesmerized in the front by Marlon Brando reciting in the story On The Waterfront."

"Are you really jumbo-ling around with your words again?
What are the words worth?" groaned the laboring philosopher who was already "heady-with-Husserll."

Meanwhile I bemused amongst the diapers and the kitten litter.
"Hmmmmmmmmmmm" I said to myself.
"Husserll can make his brain sail. Jean-Paul Sarte can give him a good argument on being and nothingness. Nietzsche can astound his mind with

expressions of insanity. Freud can con him into thinking that sex is the first *law* of life. Kant will charm him with his theories of what "is" reality. St. Thomas can soothe his ache in his savage breast for a God.

Why can't I, this little mother, put down into print the dialogue of a really existence without it being termed abstract? And we all do know what the little engine said: "I think I can !!" "I think I can!!"

Whoever said that a mother and a wife is indispensable deserves a citation for truth. What if she can't cook, she can't sew, she can't sing, and she can't decorate cakes? What is she good for?? She could be intellectually armed to safely challenge the feedbacks of the well-worn maxim:

"Children should be seen, and not heard!" Little people are mostly heard, even though not seen. When you are doing the dishes a little voice at your elbow will say: "Mom, May I have a glass of water?" As you are cooking breakfast you will answer these questions:

"Mom? Can I use your tennis racket to bounce my basketball with?"

"*Mom,* will you please listen to these 17 facts in History?"

"Mom, will you find me that red shirt that I wore last Halloween?"

"Mom? Is pop fattening?"

"Mom? Do witches have red hair?"

This is only a taste of another day in the mysterious life of the American housewife. Recently it has been propagandized by the Liberal Feminist Movement that we housewives and mothers have to fight for status and recognition.

They may have to eat their idle words. Why just the other day I walked into a second grade classroom to see the display on Our State of Texas and a charming woman said: "Whose mother is this?" A sweet little girl with a shy smile stood up and said: "That's my mother." And do you know what? She was right. I was her mother and she was my cute little girl; and the Texas Mockingbird is ever such a little bird in contrast to Alabama's state bird which is a High-Climber and has about 17 specific names.

Assuming that we all agree that it would be interesting to explore the nature of love, we hear in the background a psychologist or a prison psychatrist who is saying: "Eureka! I've found it! It is love that the human chid needs to grow emotionally, intelligently and physically!" One

Dr. psychologist wrote: "Most parents feel that if they provide: a comfortable home, food, health care, indulgent discipline, casual exposure to basic education, a world of fun, that they have fulfilled all the requirements for their children." The good Dr. went on to explain that Freddie-the-freeloader couldn't be happier. He said that you *have* to *Love* your children too. I wonder what he is trying to tell us parents?

In this book I have attempted to hit the highlights of our family dialogue hoping to probe the mysteries of human ways of thinking and to attempt to locate a grace of logic. One day I asked my four-year old why she hit the three-year old: "I hit her because she called me a blockhead first." she said. I then asked her why she scribbled on her six-year old sister's page. "I scribbled on her page because she said the orange crayon was red." she said. And then when the four-year old cried, I asked the six-year old why she hurt her: And she said: "She looked mean at me so I just hurt her a little bit."

Dear Old Dad always said, "Put up your dukes!" Gird up your Loins!
St. Polycarp, Pray for us

The only person who could choose his own Mother and Father was the Divine Person, the Son of God.

Chapter One
A Short Blunt-Edged Scream

If you were sitting and reading a prominent newspaper, would you be noticeably shocked by this glaring headline?

MEXICAN FARMER CUTS SANDALS FROM OLD TIRES

I was intrigued enough to read the article:

"Merida, Mexico (AP) - Six mornings a week, Jacinto Medina trudges several miles to work on sandals cut from discarded tires. Slung over his back are a knapsack and a small earthen jug. At his belt he carries a short, broad-bladed knife. The knife is Jacinto's most important item of property, providing a means of earning, which passes for a living here—and, in a crisis, personal defense.

With the knife, Jacinto slashes thick, spiky leaves some as long as three feet, from a henequen, or sisal, Plant.

Jacinto is a ejicatario, or communal farmer. He earns about 50 pesos, or $4.00 a week- - average for the some 60,000 henequen peasant farmers here.

Somehow he manages to provide for himself, his wife, and Five children."

Here we have found someone with whom the average American housewife can identify. She looks down briefly at her Mexican sandals, which she is ready to discard. Slunk over her back is a sack of dirty laundry and a small bottle of Bleach. At her belt she carries a short, blunt-edged scream. (Not to be heard).

The scream is one of her most important items of property, providing a means of earning which passes for a living here in the world, and, in a crisis, personal defense. With the scream, the housewife and mother slashes thick, spiky feelings of way-out insecurity. Sometimes as long as three children long. She doesn't even earn 50 pesos a week. Average earnings for the some millions of American housewives here in the world today. Somehow or other she manages to provide a home for herself, her husband spouse, and from one to children. She harbours a fondness in her heart for

Jacinto Medina who trudges several miles to work as she trudges several miles to the Supermarket, pushing a rusted stroller, with no room in it for the second trudging, stumbling hot and dusty child. Her sandals have seen better days. When she gets to the Supermarket, she has to keep her eyes averted from the more delicious looking foods, and keep to her usual basic food list.

Underneath all that daily irritations, such as the family-sized cereal boxes with enough cereal in them for two healthy-fast-eating thirteen year-old boys, we manage to foster a courageous smile. Some people say that we are crazy. Others say that only saints can foster such a smile and not be hypocrites.

With our day-old bread in hand, the one way that we can keep a brown upper crust is by bundling our bookshelves with good news. One has only to read the titles of many of us groveling-looking-women's books and you will then be able to say: "In this household sleeps a clan of saints---judging by the book titles!"

In the first book on our family bookshelf written by St. Francis de Sales, The Introduction to the Devout Life, lies a chapter that we hold dear. It handles the controversial subject of "violence" wit the utmost delicacy and discrimination. The title of the chapter is *"Of Meekness Toward Our Neighbor and Of Remedies For Anger."*

It reads as such:

"...Take care, Philothea.. it is better to find the way to live without anger, than to pretend to make a moderate use of it. It will become mistress of the place, like the serpent who easily draws in his whole body where he can once get in his head." *"But, how shall I banish anger?" you may ask me. "Some people appear to be angels in public, but are demons in their own homes. Speak all your words and do all your actions, little and great, in the mildest manner possible. This wretched life is but a journey.... with your care, take also, dear Philothea, - - A NICE HOT BATH!!"*

Many of us Catholics were not aware of the fact that Saints could have had such practical advice. We perhaps would have thought that they would tell us to sleep on a hot coal or to wear a hair shirt (a girdle is bad enough!) - to overcome our anger. For most of us, hairshirts would only multiply anger by anger. St. Francis was recognized by both Protestants and Catholics as a foremost counselor on the institution of marriage, the household, and sex-education for young people.

As a child, I was a soft touch for the sisters who love to tell of the tortures that the Saints endured. I tottered with fear for days, had nightmares, and I was filled with the wrong ideas about the saints' motives. I concluded incorrectly that if I were to ask a saint what I should do if I did not get along well in the world, that he or she would tell me to jump directly into a pot of burning oil, whereupon in the jumping I would be instantly filled with the Love of God. St. Paul is standing in the distance, motioning to us to stop.... wait! Don't jump if you lack charity! It profits you... nothing! And it profits God nothing. Even in this modern day and age, my eight year old Madeline brought home an Agnes Dei Award to me which reads:

"St. Agnes. This noble Roman virgin won the martyr's crown at the age of 13 rather than lose the treasure of her virginity. She was beheaded in 304."

This was written out in a childish cursive handwriting. It gives you the creeps to see it. (You know that they would rather be beheaded than wash the dishes or help with the cleaning on Saturday).

If you are not narrow-minded, you might enjoy reading Sam Levenson's book Everything But Money. But you might leave it muttering: "Nothing! And no money either!" Sammy used to take a brown paper bag to the movies with him on Saturday afternoons filled with black bananas, salami sandwiches, and hard-boiled eggs. Sammy was not only poor; he was very hungry. He said that he could survive through a matinee by merely sucking on one salted pretzel.

What we housewives are searching for is a book which can make us laugh. We can then continue on this wretched journey stronger in spirit and braced to face the many looming obstacles; a sink full of dirty dishes three times a day; magazine salesmen who tell you they want you to vote for them and it won't cost you any money; the telephone; the Avon lady.

I began to wash the dishes and to think of my married daughter, Ann. Ann's husband Bill is more religious than she is. Bill has fond childhood memories of being shot at while on the playground at recess time in Chicago, the Windy Hoodlum City. Not at the same time, but twenty years earlier in another big city-Cleveland, Ohio-I was jumping

rope double dutch at recess time and shouting at the top of my arched Catholic lungs:
PARROTING THE NUNS:
   Ada Backa!
   Soda Cracka!
   Ada Backa Boo!
   If your father chews
   Tobacca!
   He's a dirty Jew!!
   And—so—are—YOOUUUUU!!!

We felt required to stress the YOOUUUU!! Because all the other monkeys did and then we jumped out of the ropes usually falling and skinning our knees all gone on the concrete—for our appropriate penances.

My black son-in-law maintained his faith in a Supreme Being and he always signs his letters:

"May God continue to watch over you and bless you always.
your son,
Bill."

Our daughter Ann signs her letters:

"Solongya'bums. Whattheheckareya'doingdown

there in Texas anyway? Having any more babies? Like that,
Luv,
Ann."

In the 1980's relatives from Liverpool, England, (not Liverpool, Texas) came to visit us in Texas. It was my mother's brother Jack Herrity and his wife whom we had never met. They called me up from the bus depot.

I called up a friend and cried, "Help! Long lost relatives are here to visit and Richard is out of town! A Philosophy Professor at another University was shot and killed. He went to see about his job!" Her answer was just right. "Get out your prayer book and say some prayers." I picked them up in my car that the children call the "gray bomber". They were making a tour of the states. Their view of America from the bus was this:

"There are far too many cars and they are far too big. There is a fast food place on every corner!" When they were leaving they pronounced: "A ready made family!" Ready made? Already made? Made ready? They knew they were all ours.

A question frequently given to housewives is: DO YOU WORK? A housewife friend of mine said (without a scream) "Oh no! I sit around all day eating bon-bons!"

  Dear Old Dad always said: "Ask me no questions, I will tell you no lies!"
Gird up your loins
St. Polycarp Pray for Us

Chapter Two
Ph.d's In The Kitchen

It was the next day after the previous day and my Professor husband stepped off the stoop to begin the daily journey to his classes. Husband said: (as water seeped to his insteps) "What is this? Texas -- or the Okefenokee Swamp?" "Where is the water??" I said. I was still in shock from launching seven children to school and peered thru instant-shock eyes thru the venetians. "Why—ye gads, husband, there is a world out there my husband!" I perceived. Shielding my retinas from the sun I caught a glimpse of my backdoor neighbor bustling thru her yard with her laundry. "The world was there all the time. You are only airborne from that pot of what you call---coffee!" He said as he dropped into a chair.

At this early time of the morning our four-ager Madeline was busily doing the dishes; there is nothing children hate worse than having nothing to do. There is no greater an anguished cry heard around the world than a young child at it's mother's heart---wailing:

"What can I doooooo? Ooooooo?
"There's nothing to doooooo? Oooo?"

Our mother's problem is mainly that we are frightened to give the children a job to do because we never know where the ball will stop rolling!

My only husband was hoping to accomplish the simple and daily task of eating his breakfast. "Do you know what?" I said: "Even the bird looks half-way pretty today." I stared cautiously over at the ridiculous parakeet which we got stuck with at Christmas. In Woolworth's he or she was doing all sorts of tricks under a sign marked SPECIAL and the children and I fell in love with his or her impish grin. Two legs—but only one foot! Hence the need for all the fancy footwork! And there he or she limped. A two-legged, one-footed "con bird". "Leave it up to you to notice the bird was missing a foot." Chided the Professor.

There was no doubt in our mind that this bird was one of the Birdman's escapes. If the Society For The Prevention of Cruelty to Birds could, they would censor our thoughts, for the bird became our scapegoat for the year. There were sudden attacks thru the bars onto the cat's paws! Always on the offensive. Aggressive! Eating available bread-wrappers, putting holes into lunch bags. Steady beady-eyes! Feigning sleep!

My husband was talking and explaining to me a remark of complaint he had made earlier: "All that I said to you was, that: even though you woke up at 3am and stayed awake—that you still got eight hours of sleep!"

I pouted as I analyzed the bird-seed. "Why did you marry an Irish person if you hate the Irish so much?" "I don't hate the Irish", lied the stealthy Bohemian, "I only have said that there are none as stubborn as the Irish or as perpetually angry!"

I hit a light note: "Well, this day should not go too badly for you—I woke up your Irish-Bohemian children as I proposed to do for Lent".

"For Lent! You are supposed to wake them up—everyday!" he shouted. I bragged. "Yes, but fifteen minutes earlier for Lent! Lenten penance. Have you ever heard David talk at six-thirty in the morning?" (Can you judge all 12-ager boys by our David John?) Just touch him when he is sleeping in the morning, he flies out of his bed and turns on the speech like a clock-radio. This morning he started talking and scratching his head all over the breakfast table. He told me all about the Baylor-A & M basketball game. It seems as though one of the Baylor guys fouled up on an A & M guy and what the Baylor guy didn't know was that the Aggie football guys were lined up on the sides and…"

David's eyes popped with the Rice Krispies.

"And can I have two eggs this morning?" On and on went the descriptive discourse. I packed five lunches, lulled by the speech.

I believe in children following the leadings of their talents and their wills. (I also believe that by the sheer feat of survival--- that the parents may hopefully offer a few constructive suggestions as to their children's constructive social futures).

Twelve-ager boys are good for:

Talking out
Walking dogs
Finding dogs (or anything) and money,
Telling corner grocery store boys their
Teen-age sisters' life histories.
Kicking footballs off of bedroom walls,
Fixing telephones, doorbells, toasters,
Broken toys.

Changing light bulbs
Bringing salesmen into the kitchen,
Talking on the phone for five minutes before
Relinquishing it to it's proper owner-etc.

David was chattering on: I'm reading All-of-a-Kind-Family, Mom. Do you know why they call it All-of-a-Kind? Because they have five girls! And guess what they had at the end of the book!" I expected and braced for the worst. "A son!!" David said proudly. And then in his proudness I realized suddenly that he was not only a walking tape recorder, but also my dear little son. I was sorry that I had screamed at him before he went to school. I had bellowed:

"David! Shut up!! Long enough to EEAATTTTTT! David winced. "If you don't like me .....and you don't want me to talk....then why did you bring me into the world?"

We all just can't appreciate a little bit of twelve-ager logic and wisdom fifteen minutes before the school morning exodus. To tell the absolute truth and excluding all symbolical logic, I was not fully aware of the whole truth, that he knew that I actually did bring him into this world. My thoughts flashed back to last Sunday when we were taking our weekend drive over to the A&M Veterinarian Experimental school to see the three-legged Spanish goats. We passed a city park on the way. David yelled:

"Look! Look at the lovers!"
"Did ya' see that, Mom?"

I protested: "All I saw was a bundle of fur coats!"
"Me too! A bundle of fur! All bundled up!" David clamored.

I glanced at my husband who blushed and rolled his eyes….. After we finished feeding the deer some grass (which particular deer they had on a special diet!)….gave some cows a bad experience…..petted the mangy diseased cats… our Sunday special at Texas A&M was over and we started for home. Again David shouted:
"Remember the lovers!"

Life is always just as my father prophesied in his Liverpudlian style: "Never put of for tomorrow—what you can do today." Therefore, there is no such word as "can't". Father was not a loquacious man, but when he versed at all he did say something. You listened. Whenever I was sleeping I usually kept an ear open on his arrival: Old Dad loved me almost as much as he loved the Cleveland Shopping News. Glaring was a particular effort....so he stared at me.

He spoke:
"Children were made to be seen
Not heard. Besides! What, are you going to Be? When and where and IF you grow up??" "Errr. I don't just know what I can change into, sir" I stammered. I struggled because I floundered. Pull yourself together! My tics were ticking.

The seed was sown. I knew then that my fatalistic future would be that I would grow up certainly to be a dumb bunny!

The children were at school now and the old man of the sea (my natural husband) went off to work, shortly thereafter to return. "You thought you got rid of me? Well, I saw the mailman coming, so I came back." I couldn't resist the ensuing battle. "What's with that mailman? Everyday you say: "Did the mailman come yet? Where is the mailman? I think I hear the mailman!"

In the short while that my husband was gone I was looking up the word "potential" in the dictionary and I discovered an interesting long word. "Post hoc, ergo propter hoc." The meaning of the word is: "in logic, the fallacy of thinking that a happening which follows another, must be its result." Now that I had the Professor handy I asked him to tell what that meant----really.

"Please" the searching professor begged, "Where is my Wittengenstein?" "Tell me what 'post hoc, ergo propter hoc' means and I'll find Wittengenstein for you", challenged the efficiency plus. "That simply is and simply put: The Fallacy of False Cause". Professionally put. The fallacy of false cause!

Puffing with false pride I unwittingly tried An Aristotelian Syllogism:

"Some housewives are alcoholics. Some alcoholics are housewives. Not all housewives are alcoholics."

Perhaps because of a built-in argumentative unbalance I was foiled again!

Everyone knows that you cannot be an alcoholic and a housewife at the same time. No salesman would ever say:

"Is the Alcoholic in?" hahahahaha

Some housewives and mothers are suspected of being alcoholics because some of them drink wine with breakfast, lunch, dinner, and snack. Or would you rather knit a sock??

By this time I was peering into my dirty, burnt, corroded, decayed-with-time oven. I hastily dreamt up an out-door Indian fire with all of the children huddled around a nicely swept-out teepee. I thought of all Phyllis Diller's jokes about dirty ovens. I visualized an Indian husband who would have respect for his squaw and who would NEVER slap me on the belly and say:

"Do you know what you need?
What you need is to get out!
Out of the wigwam!! Meet real people!
Spend real money. (Get away from Monopoly!)
Find out what is really going on in the real world."

Husbands do that you know. He forgets he told me that the Professors mottos is: KEEP 'EM BAREFOOT AND PREGNANT!" Many business executives are unaware of the fact that many housewives are slapped on the belly line daily and on the rear-end with the fictional ad-lib:

"When are you going to start taking the PILL?"

by many well meaning, obese, doughty, and undesirable people.

Old-fashioned mamas don't have the anxieties that Harvey Cox says readers of Playboy have. Their persistent anxieties that they may mix a drink incorrectly, enjoy a jazz group that is passe', or wear last year's necktie style tyrannizes them. But mommas are tyrannized by a greater force that drives up through the boob tube as they stay-at-home in their seductive manner. Just last night I went into the recreation room to tack up some winterizing plastic (Spokane) when the dialogue from the TV drove me back upstairs, in a tyrannical fashion. The scene came through as a group of teenagers on an island---one of the girls had been raped and the girls wanted a law passed on the Island to protect the girls.

The boys, however, felt that the law was an insult to their integrity. The girl, who was raped, couldn't remember the date that she got raped on. "What's in a date?", she asked. "I'll be that you cannot even remember today's date!" I rushed up the stairway before our ten year old could ask: "What does rape mean?" Dear Old Dad Never talked about rape. Dear Old Dad (D.O.D.) could only say: "A stitch in time saves nine!" Or...... he would never allow any criticism. Dear Old Dad would always say: "Were you there, Charlie?" And there is a Ph.d. needed in the kitchen.

There are some secure parents who write books about the loose habits of young people. "Mr. Tom Buck, who married a lovely Pat Kernahan, and together they begat eleven lovely children" wrote in his book:

all about fast cars
fast women with short skirts
dumb boys with tight pants
Heavy drinking plus heavy breathing...
Which equals= no conversation.

They label it "the art of lost conversation." (David doesn't have it yet!) I almost get to the conclusion that housewives and mothers were indispensable and now I rediscover that we are the mothers and the breeders of fast women, dumb boys, heavy drinking, and the lost art of conversation. We are so human that it is sickening and very disheartening. Does this mean that the Feminist Movement may have the whole show to run?? In their progressive philosophy for women, they do away with fathers after the fathers give them the "joy" of being a mother. Then put the kidlets into nurseries at age four weeks and take them out of school at age twenty-one. What do their kids do?? They no doubt promote long skirts, drive slow cars, and talk all day and talk all night. They don't even need fathers anymore. To save time, you can have artificial insemination and Ann Landers points out in her column that you may have very intelligent fathers at that. Blonde headed medical students, if you prefer.

Only God can make a tree and figure out women too. I came back to a real portion of my life as I stood---bent over as usual, examining my blitz-stricken, over-worked oven. A voice boomed through the rust. A halo of rust formed in my hair.

The voice boomed.
More rust let go.
"GET A JOB!"

The voice beat a hasty retreat into the cruelest of all tormentors, the Texas Sun. Sartes's Being and Nothingness got to him and gave him a nothing complex. "He doesn't love me because I don't have a Ph.d and I'm not the hostess with the mostest… not even the canoeing' I sighed. The rust slipped around my ears then.

Are They All Yours?

Who else would spend time losing weight but a housewife? Donna Massey lost 34 pounds. She said: "I seemed doomed to be obese, doughty and an undesirable housewife." You never heard of a doughty undesirable History Professor have you? The truly successful housewife is only seen in person on the boob tube. Wriggling around in silk pajamas, smoking (of course) a cigarette, drinking a drink (of course) and flanked on both sides by a maid and/or a cook; making hilarious quips which came from her own imagination to break up the maid and/or cook; perversely making snide remarks about her husband and children with her conscience being that of a contemporary age style. Perfect. People stay up late at night to watch her and to sympathize with her.

In an enlightened moment of truth, I saw the whole created nass of humanly unpremeditated ordinary housewives standing up to their knees in Ajax cleaners. No longer are they finding their identities through their children, they are instead feverishly realizing themselves through their husband's Ph.d's. They have been relentlessly and unresistently putting them through colleges and universities. They have been losing sleep nursing their babies and their doctoral dissertations. They have been burdened with dictionaries of all languages.

I have it dialogued authentically from one housewife that while she helped to educate her husband, her own English went to the dogs.

"I don't know what it is all about!!" she nursed a flagrant scream.

"The Dean of Engineering tried to explain it to us at a meeting. I think that John is going to earn some money some day when he gets through. And that's good enough for me!!"

Some women have said to me: "What does your husband know? All he knows is what he gets out of books!"

The more fortunate and enlightened wives are those wives of professors who are professors themselves—to make books meet!!!

Right about this time of the day my contemporaries around the world are standing in their kitchens cursing the inventors of ovens and high cupboard shelves and dreaming of the day when they can go back to college. Their voices in chorus (Old Greek) blend and resound all around the world like one huge omen:

"I've got a degree in kitchen sinks!! Ha!" sings the first witch.

"I've got a D.D. Degree! In Dirty Diapers! Ha. Ha. Sings the second witch.

"I get the third degree every time I burn the coffee!!" hahaha sings the third witch.

(And B.A. stands for Busy Alright!!)

The Professor told me that a Ph.D. means "Pile it higher and deeper!"

A most hackneyed question that has been put to me many times in the past forty years is:

"Where did you come from?"
"Where did you go?" (For the past twenty years). For the lay people this means "Which University did you attend?"
Why—we obese, doughty and undesirable housewives are so very frightened! One fine day when my husband and I were standing somewhere, a man came up to ask my husband questions about his work. The man then looked at me with a look that said he hoped it would make me disappear. His look was not working. All of a sudden I blurted out, "I'm from the SCHOOL OF HARD KNOCKS!" His look did not change, but my new husband let out a tremendous laugh that I haven't heard since.

One very saintly female smile with a Ph.D said to me in a condescending manner as she patted me on the head:

We have a new status for you housewives, you are a homemaker. We love you just the way you are. Don't change." As she continued with her monologue I did some quick thinking. "Don't change!?" She loves us just the way we are? Dirty ovens? Fast cars? Dumb kids? Kids with short skirts, tight pants, their own thing? NO MISSIONARY SPIRIT?"

She consoled me further: "Yes, you housewives are something that you don't find in books. You have something that you do not find in books."

I was standing behind a batter of baking powder biscuits as she spoke and I eyed her simple soul-life suspiciously. As I counted out two teaspoonfuls of baking powder (the double-acting powder) I braved to say: "What is that?" (I knew that it wasn't cooking, as such, because I had already eaten her cooking and it was far superior to mine. All successes included). I secretly hoped that it would be sex-appeal.

"Love!" was her dramatic reply.

And she breathed so hard with romantic feelings that the baking powder did not want to identify with the flour and my consciousness was flooded with the hard core of reality of general statements. But I did ponder the issue and I did agree with her. I have never seen a book love. That part was true.

Our husband's educations are rubbing off on some of us however:

Our service people such as the milkman, the paper boy, the avon lady have to suffer with such remarks offhand as these at times:

"I'm sorry. I can't take any milk as yet. I have to take a survey to see what my neighbors are taking. Your milk is good, as such, however."

"I'm sorry Avon lady—not today can I make a purchase. You see we have articles ad infinitum ad nauseum---- there is no exit!"

As for you dear paper boy, I shall take no paper. St. Thomas says: "The mind is loftier than the body" ipso facto, I shall take great care! If you will!"

If you live through raising children-----you may become somewhat of a celebrity because of them! Friends of mine who raise large families are always being photographed and interviewed. The interviewer interviews the young mother who "remembered to put pins in her head the night before". As the questions come to issue the children in the environment proceed to mingle and maul. Now the interviewer begins:

"Whatsa' matter? Do you mean that you actually feed all these kids?"

It is the little mothers turn to brag. "Three meals a day! Plus sixteen snacks! Of course (tee hee) we eat a lot of hamburger, tee hee". Whilst unbeknown to the little mother the interviewer cannot afford much more himself.

The interviewer begins his morbid curiosity program:

"Do you do their dirty laundry?"
Betcha' have a lot of dirty laundry??"

"Do you laugh at their jokes?"
Betcha' hear the same joke over and over!"

"Do you make their pants tighter for them? Do you give the baths?"

Betcha' wish that you had three bathrooms!
Heh, heh, heh.
Who fixes their hair?
Bet it costs you a fortune to have their teeth fixed.
Do any of them wear glasses? Contacts? Braces?
I'll betcha' have a lot of doctor bills!"

And he rounds up his interview with a question that seemingly is more his business than it is yours.

"Does your husband want any more children?"

The poor interviewer is beginning to look ill. Mother fixes him a cup of Hills Bros. After all, he's only human!

One Professor Richard T.A. Coleman, a noted journalist and teacher of writing says:

"Who cares that people's minds and spirits have withered away??"

The common-ordinary everyday housewife cares that people's minds and spirits have withered away. In her small confused way she knows that there is a fly in the ointment. This solves the mystery for many of why she stays at home and curses the oven instead of roaming off to foreign lands looking for land-minded Richard Burtons. They really do care. Through a lot of faults of hers she may be the cause of the people's withered spirits and false minds and tight pants, but that does not lessen the care, nor the spirit of care. We do try in our own withered emancipated human ways to do well with loving and the living with peoples. I ask you casually with great aplomb—who else could live with:

Play dough and bubble-gum, crayons, dolls, straws, firecrackers, play money, dolls that pee, burp, and cry: bubbles, slingshots, rubber bands, bobby pins, instant coffee, chips, crackers, cake mixes, lonesome salesmen, Jehovah witnesses (just as lonely); garage sales, dog, cats, birds, burnt toast, tradeo programs, high cupboards, low broilers, candy cigarettes, balloons, high chairs, cereal gimmicks, portable potties, piggy banks, teddy bears, baseballs, footballs, crying, belching, cinnamon toast, sleezy curtains, dirty floors, ripped pants, artificial flowers, fertile cats, nosey kids, noisy kids, dirty ovens, empty wine bottles, lots and lots of trash, soggy lettuce, weak celery, "I wanna' hold your haannnnndddd!!!" records, broken glasses, broken teeth; fights for left-over cake batters; sprung ball-point pens, dull pencil sharpeners, handle-less screwdrivers, over-due postage, small sinks, over-sized plugs, loose hammer heads, tons and tons of excuse notes for teachers; school papers to sign, PTA-PTO meetings to haunt; (Parents Turned Apathy).

Only the multi-dimensional mother and father can love the Realities of the Sick Society.

One very hot and sunny day in Detroit when I was still a young mother and learning the ropes of diplomacy, I had my growing family at a playground. A woman stood watching us for quite a while as she leaned against the swing set for support. I was undertaking the herculean task of entreating talkative David who was then only a chattering three-ager—into getting off of the glistening silver slide which by now was a burning slice of steel! I coaxed him: "Come on Davie. We will all have a nice cold glass of lemonade." The woman watching us began to sneer at us and walked away in disgust leaving the words behind her to me:

"Oh! Bribe 'em to be good, eh!!"

"Are we poor, Mom?" asked David when he was twelve.

I said, "No. Why do you ask me that?"

"Well, when I told Dad that I gave my allowance to the poor, he said that we are the poor?"

"Well, Dad is right—he has a lot of bills to pay and it costs $4000 a year just to feed this growing family. Then he gives $17.00 a month in allowance money to you children—and then you give it to the poor. If you want to give it to someone---give it back to your Dad so he can buy himself some matching socks."

David said, "Sister says to give our pennies to the missions." His brother Rick said he knew we were not poor because we could drink milk between meals and the O'Briens, who had eight children, had to drink water. He did not know that his Dad owed the milkman $500 dollars.

In the 1970's our children kept saying that all those years we were eating healthy when healthy wasn't cool. Our main menu was baked chicken, rice, and salad. Lately at school, Madeline found out what other families had for their menu---frito pies, chili cheese dogs, pizza, and fried chicken. I found out 20 years later that the children at school had 20 dollar bills in their pockets and were ordering fast foods delivered to them at lunch!

A school bus full of basketball and football players from our rich parish went down south to play against a poor parish team. When they left from there, the other team gave them peanut butter and jelly sandwiches to eat on their way back.

On the way back, they threw their sandwiches out the windows and had the driver stop at McDonalds.

Dear Old Dad never said the word poor. He always said, "You should eat your dessert first so that you will be sure to get it!"
Gird up your loins
St. Polycarp Pray for Us!

Chapter Three
Why Philosophy?

With insight fashion, Rudyard Kipling caught a picture of the close relationships of children and parents with these four lines:

"I have eaten your bread and salt.
I have drunk your water and wine.
The deaths ye died, I have watched beside,
And the lives ye led---------were mine!"

I don't like to discuss the unknown, like fifteen and sixteen-ager daughters, but when you have a houseful of them, what choice do you have?

I was in the kitchen in my usual spot, pitting brains against brawn, challenging the Dream Whip and fretting at the bird, when my sixteen-ager daughter Therese, unzipped her shorts, rolled down her underwear to below her gaping navel, and said to me:

"This is where my new bathing suit will come to. Honestly, Mom, no one wears them way up to their waists anymore! Besides, those kind make you look much fatter too!"

I was later to console myself with the fact that it was not a bikini's bikini; however, I did wonder what Grandma would have done in such a similar situation, not to mention Grandpa. No doubt she and he would have buttoned the sixteen-ager's lip. Grandma and Grandpa were tough characters to put us modern weaklings to shame. The styles that society was setting or the clothes that the "gang" was wearing did not put any gray hairs on Granny.

Like a muse, I mused: "O.K. dear, it's your ugly navel that's going to be showing and not mine. You can always put a large bean in it." "Mother, really---we can't wear the old-fashioned suits you wear, way up to ---here!" and she throttled herself very dramatically.

Who are they who say that children imitate their parents?? That daughters take after their Moms? I cannot sew a straight seam and my three oldest daughters sew their own clothes. I wouldn't be seen dead or alive in a bathing suit. I wash my hair with dish detergent.

As I cut up the chickens I let my thoughts loll

back to my sixteens; if I had been in the same situation and was asking Dear Old Dad if my bathing suit was too skimpy, his admonition would have been quite pertinent to the situation:

Dear Old Dad would have said: "How many beans make five? Or better yet: "All dressed up and no place to go!"

That was Dear Old Dad who married the girl who married Dear Old Dad. When the angel of death took Jack Mapother by the hand—Jack might have said to the angel: "Oh! Would that I could smell the River Mersey just once more!" The gentle Angel might have spoken a kind word. I imagined the angel used one of Dear Old Dad's maxims:

"All work and no play
Made Jack a dull boy.
Come with me to the Eternal Playground, Jack."

And Jack went with Him for he never ever wanted "to put off for tomorrow what he could do today". If I could have stayed the Angel's hand I certainly would have, for part of my embryonic heart went with him. No longer could I spend my evenings watching Jack taking a busman's holiday by reading the Cleveland Shopping News. As a linotype operator and proofreader he would scan the pages---stopping now and then to emote dramatically:

"Blazes! Look at that typographical error!
If you want anything done right
You have to do it yourself!"

One time Dear Old Dad had to leave the Shopping News for a time due to illness and they presented him with a wrist watch. He held it up to me in the air and cried real tears. "I've worked for them for fifteen years and look what they gave me, and I've loved them!" Certainly I was at a loss for words for I knew that material things couldn't replace love given and I was surprised in my young age that he expected more from a Company Inc.

When Dad left this world after a life filled with aphorisms, my favorite: "Enough is as good as a feast") I again imagined that his conversation with God went something like this:

God: "Oh, there you are Johnny. I've loved you very much."

Johnny: "I'm sorry, I think that I forgot about Your Existence now and then. What is one man's meat is another man's poison."

God: "Just the same Johnny, I've loved you since you emerged from your mother's womb. Come in. There's always room for one more."

Johnny: "Fancy that. I guess it takes all kinds to make up the world. I'm coming Lord. For what is sauce for the goose, is sauce for the gander."

I wonder what my single parent-father would say today seeing me the mother of a large and growing family. I have heard it said that he was his mother's child! Dear Old Dad always said: "The more the merrier!" Some psychologists are telling us that we are out of style. I know that we are out of money. "Two child families are all that women can truly handle." They prophesy from the decks of their yachts. I say back to the psychologists who hold this theory - - I say it from the deck of the worn kitchen floor:

"Prove it. Prove that I do not have enough time in one day to love equally my ten kids---time to live and time in which to let live!"

"…Well, for one thing you always get our underpants mixed up!" growled a contentious fourteen-ager. At Christmas, 1968, I had an idea. I bought Sun., Mon., and Tues., panties. Would that solve my mixed-up career?

1ˢᵗ voice answered: "Hey! You've got my Tuesday!"
2ⁿᵈ voice replied: "I do not! Besides, this is only Monday!"

Famous Dr. Lieberman valiantly said—and I quote:

"Children from large families often suffer from a sort of maternal deprivation. The day's length remains the same, and parental attention is spread thin."

Dr. Lieberman missing the head of the nail by a mile should have said was that there are not enough brains and wit to spread around to keep up with all the glowing ideas that one teenager can develop. A bright asset of a smaller family is that there are not so many people around to tell the mother and father what to do and there are also less people around to tell the mother and father what they are going to do. Dr. Lieberman's theory wouldn't hold with an internationally recognized composer, musician, poet, writer, film maker and a great still-photographer who was Gordon Park the fifteenth little Parks and who worships " the every memory of his mother who had died when he was 16." While she lived, she was his inspiration filling his head with strange and noble thoughts, and gave him an unbounded faith in himself as a human being.

Many of us often wonder. Why Philosophy? In fact, why any thinking at all? I picked up one of my husband's exam papers to stimulate the powers of my brain.

To quote: "Which one of the following illustrates an invalid conversation?

1) "Some beverages are stimulants to "Some stimulates are beverages."
2) "All peripatetics are philosophers" to "All philosophers are peripatetics."
3) "Some scholars are teachers" to "Some teachers are scholars."
4) "No pterodactyl is a resident of the Brooklyn Zoo" to "No resident of the Brooklyn Zoo is a pterodactyl."
5) None of these.

First of all we must know what an invalid conversion is and that is why children got to college to study philosophy. I, for one, consider myself as an invalid conversion which may account for the way in which I handled the following situation:

It was a Sunday afternoon and this Sunday housewife had her head in the usual place - - - the jaws of the oven and I was expertly analyzing one berry-pie dripping from the other. It was not the heat but the breathing of three girls which brought my attentions to people, places and things. Two of the girls were mine and one was the girl next door.

They were speaking to me which accounted for the rumbling and dust exposure. "We don't have anything to dooooooo. So, we are going to see The Night They Raided Minskys at the Local Palace." It was a challenging statement and it was a 'limpin' lump o' brick-dust to the rescue." "Oh, no, you're not!" it was my voice that spoke. I braved the fire "with bullets kickin' dust-spots on the green" They spoke: "Why not?" (Dr. Spock said that when they were three and four ager I didn't have to give them reasons for everything. That was eleven years ago.) Carefully disengaging my head from the oven's cramped enclosure I said:

"Because The Night They Raided Minskys is a dumb picture with a lot of dumb grown-ups running around doing a lot of dumb things."

"Did you see it?" asked a cautious fourteen-ager peering out at me from behind cascades of beautiful brunette hair. "No" said I. The stared at me. Three in a row. I thought of playing patti-cake patti-cake but stared back at them instead. "When the cartridges ran out, you could hear the front ranks shout, Hi!! Ammunition - - mules, an' Gunga Din!" My front rank fears were turned into smiles of grace.

Said the first voice: "First we are going to walk the dog.

"Then we are going to bake some brownies." Assured the second voice.

And the third voice of creative wisdom and teenage endeavor said: "Then we will finish sewing our spring dresses!"

My heart overflowed with a goodly theme as I sang my ode to the King and par soap suds flowed over the dishes and I realized that not every teenage heart lie in planned rebellion. Not every moment!!!

Dr. Joseph S. Roucek blamed the disintegration of family life on a number of factors:

1. divorce
2. abdication of the roles assigned by nature

3. puritanical sex attributes
4. status-seeking
5. and integration with the American way of life.

On a busy day in a normal household environment without much in the way of an introduction, my husband and I were arguing over whose children our children were:

"For they are yours!" said the husband.
"For they are yours!" echoed the wife.

Taking her cue a voice belonging to 14-ager, Irene, called from the bathroom,

"I don't belong to no one! I am myself! I belong to myself! I can do what I want to do! Where is my allowance?"

No parent really expects their children to grow up so fast. To drive so soon! To eat so much! To wear so many clothes! To need glasses so often, contacts, braces, and graduation rings so soon!

In an article by Bernice L. Lifton entitled "The High Cost of Graduation" we read:

"Individual expenses for senior activities in many suburban schools average over $200. Barberton, Ohio graduates also find a formal prom inadequate, so 500 docile parents worked weeks to follow it with a six-course banquet, complete with name band entertainers. Some parents even added champagne parties or trips abroad. And each year the clamour grows for more."

An early morning dialogue (7 O'clock) in the year 1968 with Johnny, my 18-ager nephew, whom I had not seen in seven years is not to be forgotten. He searched through cupboards high and low, through the refrigerator and then the oven. The conversation went as follows:

Johnny: "Whats good to eat for breakfast, Aunty Irene?"

I fell right into his trap because I was determined to make my answer very heroic indeed, very nourishing, not to mention very exciting.

Aunty Irene: "There is dry cereal, cooked cereal, coffee (instant or perked), milk, orange juice (fresh or frozen or Tang), bacon, sausages, pancakes or waffles, toast, cinnamon rolls, ham and eggs…"

At that the teenager leaned on the cupboard and hung his head:

"Aww, you sound just like my mother!'

Needless to say, the boy-child was disappointed. In my great pride and haste to be popular, I blew the test. He had looked to me for a Bird of Paradise and found the state of Stupidity. Weeks later I realized that he had wanted me to say: "Want a good breakfast Johnny? Drink a glass of vinegar and read a good book!"

Because from the sink and in my spirit "He lifted up my head, and he plugged me where I bled, and 'e guv me harf-a-pint O' water green. It was crawlin' and stunk, But of all the drinks I've drunk, I'm gratefullest to one from----Gunga Din!" (Kipling)

I was busy preparing a luncheon and a voice broke into my reverie time. "Hey, Moms! When are we going to get a new stove? This oven is a gas! Don't tell me I have to boil my eggs on this ancient relic?" 16-ager Therese entered the scene, she was recognizeable by pierced ears, shaded eyelids, neutral contacts framing large beautiful blue eyes. She spoke again:

"Hmm, just finished my exercises,

Eggs are wonderful for diets.
Don't feed me anything fattening.
My hair looks long today, doesn't it?
Did you see those little old ladies in church?
Looks like they just got their hair done and then slept on it.

I got a B on my French exam.
Where is my new ring?
I saw the Professor in church who played in the play The Mousetrap. It was horrible.
He really looks like that!
Babysitting is money toughly earned.
Where is Dad?
Don't tell me he got away again!"

This is the end of the noontime quote as she ate her hard-boiled eggs to be followed by a candy bar.

When Therese was four years old she was playing in front in Detroit with Willie Richardson. He had asked her a question. Willie's dad, David Richardson, was walking home from the University of Detroit but did not hear the question. He only heard Therese's answer.

She said, "I don't know, Willie. Only God knows and He is not telling anybody." That may be the answer to all of our mysteries.

When Therese was 16 years old, her friends poked fun of her for having so many siblings. Her retort to them was, "THEY'RE ALL I'VE GOT!"

I know of some people who dearly love large families. Sears and Roebucks for instance. And dear old Monty-Wards. My husband's philosophy professor friend who lives in Los Angeles wrote to us:

"Sears now owns my soul,
Just bought my two teenagers a motorcycle
Motor bikes for the middle group,
Bikes and trikes for the younger set.
Los Angeles swings you that way.
I can't afford to buy a car.
Marjorie took all the kids to Sears for shoes.
When is it all going to end?"
Philosophically yours:
The Delaneys, California-side.

All milkmen love families of any size and they may warn you of all the hazards of drinking dry instant milk. Our past milkmen always drove a Cadillac (he owned the milk company.) All that Dr. Delaney has is a sore bottom from riding his kid's motorcycle.

One memorable day my husband bought ice skates and skis for the whole family from—Sears. It is so easy. Just yell:

"CHARGE---IT!!"

Supermarkets' owners certainly do not want a family of any size or nationality to disintegrate. Who buys all the day-old bread and pasteries?? The canned goods without the labels??? The bags ad infinitum of rotten oranges, grapefruits, and potatoes marked "Special". Who buys the meat turning blue and marked for "Quick Sale!"???? You can hear the quiet whispers. "Someone with a big family can use those".

"Ohhhh, they're all rotten!" moaned a disillusioned fifteenager as she eyed the baby octupii. "There's a few good ones!" the philosopher philosophized, taking a busman's holiday. "It's fun to pick them out!" "Ohhh, why can't we be rich and have cupboards full of pop and potato chips like the people I babysit for?" dreamed the fourteen-ager. We have lived on kool-aid and pop-corn for twenty years, fearing to break the spell.

"Look at that!! Five pounds of rotten bananas!" shrieked the fifteen-ager. "They are a little far gone" admitted the head of the heart of the home. "But the guy ahead of me put that bag back. He already had a bagful and I guess that he did not want to look greedy". I visualized all the banana bread and banana cake ahead of me. "What you mean to say is that too much rotten bananas is too much. And while we are complaining for real, I would like to add that we are forever blocking the store aisles weighing the canned goods from hand to hand "while you" – (I pointed at the man eating a banana) "you proofread and edit every canned-good label. Take 16 small cans you say, the large can is a big gyp. Last week the woman at the Safeway said:

"WHY DON'T YOU LEAVE YOUR HUSBAND AT HOME WHEN YOU SHOP. THAT'S WHAT I DO!!
(She helped me pick up the creamed corn I knocked down while putting cans of corn back).

"I wish that Richard were home" moaned the fourteen-ager. We always had lots of apple pies when he was here". Suddenly my mind became occupied with thoughts of my eighteen-ager son. I remember distinctly some people saying about other people:

"His mother wanted him to be a doctor, so he hadda be a doctor. What he really wanted to be was a movie star."

"My husband is a lawyer.
He never wanted to be a lawyer.
He always wanted to be an engineer.
But his uncle was a lawyer.
So he hadda' be a either a lawyer or a farmer.
He still hates it!"

Dialogues matching this one are confusing. How many people like to do what they have to do?

Rick was deciding what he was going to do. "I'm gonna' be a cowboy in Montana" said the growing, growling lad. "He's gonna' rope those poor little doggies" I whispered into the date-bar mixture. "He's gonna' shoe horses and mend fences and—I wish that I was there!" drooled the reading professor.

I recalled what I had read about the father of St. Francis of Assissi. Petre' Bernadone was just furious when his son Francis wanted to run off to become a Saint. "You bum you'," he foamed. Parents can't appreciate their children, their ways and their personalities to their fullest.

It is not as though we do not have our son Richard at our fingertips. Anytime that I wanted to I could call MacGregor Lake 26. It began to sound to me like the title of a novel, "MacGregor Lake 26." "You have to go in first, before you can go out again, on that one" said the Montana operator to the Texas operator. "What is that MacGregor Lake 26?" asked the Texas operator. "It's a telephone number!" reasoned the Montana operator. I heard the response as she finally put the call through. "Sorry, all we can reach today is the schoolhouse. Call back another day."

On another day I might reach him if:
1. he is not out in the fields (where he seemingly was from 4:30 a.m. to 9p.m.)
2. if he was not asleep in the bunkhouse where there was no phone.

One night I called at 9:30 p.m. While screaming at the top of our lungs because of old connections, the conversation went like this:

"Hellooooooh!"
"Hello! Is Richard there?"
"Who?"
"Richard!"
"Oh—you mean cowboy Rick!"

"Yeah, he's here, but he's sleeping now and there is no phone in the bunkhouse."

"Oh. Well, did he get my electric blanket?" (I was living in Texas and spent time watching the temperatures in Montana drop to 15 degrees below!) The voice answered: "Can you call back tomorrow?" "Sure thing. It's not important. Just his mother in Texas." No one seemed any the wiser.

One real day I finally reached Richard. He said: "Hey! What do you guys want anyway?"

In the 1990's a lady came into the church's gift book store where I worked. She told me that she had ten children. I told her that I also had ten. I then asked her how many girls versus boys. She answered: 7 boys and 3 girls. I said: "Seven boys! Oh No! I have 8 girls and 2 boys. She answered: "Eight girls! Oh No!" (God works in mysterious ways).

She shared her life with me on a tape she made and we became good friends. Dolores Rike had been a nurse during World War II on the planes that brought gasoline to General Patton. One time the planes almost had to crash and the co-pilot started to cry. She comforted him by saying, "Don't cry… .I'm praying the rosary and everything is going to be ok."

Dolores did not know that someday she would be co-creator with God of ten unpremeditated human existences! Her future husband, Col. James C. Rike, had to fly his some kind of glider for three more years before they could get married. His glider is now in a museum in Germany.

Dear Old Dad always said, "All ashore that's going ashore!"
Gird up your loins
St. Polycarp Pray for us!

Chapter four
Can You Remember All Their Names?

I was put on earth to bring back dirty clothing in a clean condition? This is precisely why housewives have been using that blunt-edged scream at their belts for all of these years . Ah, hah! A scream of self-defense:

One well known woman has said:
"The contraception revolution as well as the Industrial Revolution has caused women to lose their identities."

Women have been screaming since Eve ate the apple. If the American housewife needs an excuse for a faceless status, what then are the excuses for the men and women in all of the other professions?

Why is it that Eve was not surprised to hear a snake talk?

For centuries now housewives have been running around like chickens with their heads cut off. Before Christ, and even in the time of Christ, we hear history echo His words: "Martha, Martha, thou art careful and troubled about many things!" Women have been serving mankind spasmodically. Up at 6, down at 11. Serving meals for four or for fourteen. Until 10 o'clock in the morning "Moms" has answered these particular and same questions four times or fourteen:

"Mom!"
"Mom!" (You would prefer maybe "Beautiful?") Mom! Where's the tape? The scissors? My blue socks with the orange stripes? White socks? My white blouse?"
"Mom! Got a pencil? A tea bag? An eraser? A pen? (It has to be a black pen) Fifteen cents?

"Wife! Are my eggs cooked like rocks yet?"
"Wife! What's burning?"

Hurry, hurry, mom, we'll be late for the world and you will never be voted the mother of the year.

"Hey, Mom! The baby peed on the floor!
"Mom! There is a salesman at the door!
"Now he is in the living room, Mom!"
Hurry up Mom, now the children are asking him questions: They are asking him:

"Is that your pen?
Where did you get it?
Where did you get your pants?
You've got shoes just like Daddy.
Are you a Daddy?"

The valiant little woman scurries through the breakfast litter to rescue the already languishing salesman. (Who now wishes that he had gone to see A Streetcar named Desire instead of going to work!) He doesn't appear too much the worse for the wear, but harbors now a suspicious look. He remembered what he came for, and like the children - - starts to ask a lot of questions. Instead of Mom he calls her "Mam." You can imagine what a relief that is for Mom.

And the Salesman said to the Mom:
"Do you like classical music, Mam?"

At 9' o'clock in the morning?

Hmmmm. Mom thought of her five-cent garage sale record with Sir Malcolm Sargent conducting the Liverpool Philharmonic Orchestra. If you are not from Liverpool you couldn't really appreciate Hungarian Dance No. 5 played by Liverpudlians, nor truly relax to Overtures to Yeomen of the Guard and Patience". Mother spoke

"I've got Mozart in the study."

"Loving You Has Made Me Bananas" in the teen-agers room. "Lord, You Gave Me One Mountain Too Many" in the twelve-agers room. Burl Ives singing "a little red snake wriggling on the water" in the kiddies' bedroom."

The salesman left physically and mentally exhausted before Mom could answer his question, "Do you like classical music, Mam?"

Just the day before, the Fuller-Brush man sold Mom a "can of what you get another can of half-price." Mom could hear her husband's voice in her subconscious. "Don't buy anything from the Fuller-Brush man - - it's cheaper at the Supermarket!"

And the Fuller-Brush man said: "I have a big family too."
And Mom asked: "What parish are you in?"
Salesman: "We are not Catholics. We are Lutherans. You don't have to be a Catholic to have children."
The salesman and Mom laughed and laughed. He said that his oldest daughter would deliver the spray wax next week and the children kept bugging Mom

to tell them what was so funny!

"What you need; what you really need as a person is to go to the beauty parlor" cautioned a well-meaning cousin of mine on a sunny day. What I am trying to tell you is that because you are a housewife people can talk to you like this and you must remain humble so are not to muddy up the waters. They would never caution a female Professor of English to go to a beauty parlor. Rather they would say:
"I need to go somewhere with you if you are a Professor."

I answered: "Do they sell beauty there? Actually I find beauty a hazard!"

A beauty parlor is one of those parlors where women come out of after spending $7.00 out of their grocery money just to hear themselves say:

"I can't wait to get home and change my hairdo! I just don't feel like myself!"

Even though they have drooled for hours over Elisabeth Taylor Burton and her great lovely beautiful purple eyes, they do not want anyone trying to make them look like her.
"Who ya trying to kid?" They ask with suspicion,

That ain't me. And I know it."
(What is a Brobdingnagian bosom?)

"Mom! We don't have any school tomorrow!"
"Mom said: "Isn't that wonderful? We can all play ring around the rosie; button button; play nurse; play school; play office; and play house.

Besides matching socks, which no housewife has yet been able to do efficiently; one housewife wrote an entire article on the art of finding lost socks; we are also supposed to be helping our children discover their basic identities. After all of these years of what some of our predecessors have called "slavery", we have produced a "lost" generation. Thousands upon thousands of hours were spent washing diapers, dishes, ovens, wall, floors, faces, arms, legs, windows; but they tell us that without love it profited us nothing.

John Steinbeck has had bad news for us. He said in an interview for TEMPO, Houston Chronicle, March, 1969.

"But I've never seen a time when the country was so confused as to where it is headed. The trouble with the young people seems to be that they are trying to swing the wheel around and take off in the opposite direction."

Some parents are supporting hippy children. It gives the parents a false feeling of security to do this.

They fear, they may do something worse than just leaving their homes and slobbing around. (John Steinbeck quoted also that he feared for their laziness.) You know these children have come out of homes run by common-ordinary, obese, doughty, undesirable housewives turned homemakers who at some time or other (and most of the time) have given up, gone without, and scrubbed to the very marrow of the universe, instead of "sharing" the work!

What is there about wifeing the house that could cause one to lose one one's personal identity thereby hosting others to lose their identities and now everyone has to go out and look for themselves? Perhaps it is THE SPIRIT in which a wife to the house chases the DUSTBALLS. Or it may be SIMPLY AND FACTUALLY an open display of FREE WILLS.

A well - meaning mother could lose her mind by the time she finishes reading The House That

Jack Built. By the time that you've eaten the malt that killed the rat that kissed the maiden with the crumpled horn--you are ready to kill the vicar who married the two slobs.

Everyone is home but Jack. Like all good-intentioned Dads everything lay in the house that Jack built---except Jack. And meanwhile back at the ranch the old lady has a group of sadistic children who are clapping their little perfectly-formed hands together in an enchanting tone:

"Read it again, Mom!!
"Read it again!!"

The obese, doughty, undesirable housewife wishes she had a dragoon of wine. Who chased the dog? Who married the cat? Who tricked the rat? Who got drunk on the malt? Who? Who? Who?

Book publishers from their sleezy yachts murmur: "The children love it, that's who. Print more, more and more reprints." The mothers are on a crazy trip. If she dares to drink in between meals anything besides water they call her an alcoholic or a coffee-holic. So stories like this have to be saved until bedtime!!

With the freedom of press in our country there are articles printed which call housewives and mothers obsolete and over-eating people. An article in the Houston Post read as follows:

"The Obsolete Wife: She overeats or (should it be and/or?) Smother-loves her children."

'The women Libbers invented the term smother-love. The written article went on to say:

"Men are wedded to their careers,
The wife is a mistress who gets what is left."
What I want to know is what is left? What is left? What is left for the housewife mistress?? What is??
A sadistic smile.

Another article written by a director of a divorce court reconciliation said:

"There are many happy little girls hiding out in suburbia posing as grown-up women. They're scared!! They sleep until noon! They busy themselves in whiskey, hot fudge sundaes, or the bridge club."

Eight years ago my then eleven-ager daughter called to me from down the hallway:

"Hey Moms! Where is my yellow printed blouse? I put it in the laundry four days ago and it didn't come back yet?" "Come back?
Come back from where?" I thought. The realization

that I am the laundry is not my favorite cup of tea. I can rationalize that when J.P. Morgan says to his secretary: "Mrs. Smith, where is my customs report? I gave it to you to type yesterday and it didn't come back yet."---that she knows that she is just a typewriter to him. But a mother begs for a more cozy relationship. In fact, it is essential.

This is why housewives have been using that blunt-edged scream at their belts. A scream of self-defense. The scream that can be heard around the world in any language.

My contemporaries and I are so busy changing diapers and stirring up Gorilla milk for lunches that we haven't even heard of the happy little housewives in Suburbia who are hiding out and gorging on booze and hot fudge.

Mrs. Thecla McCarthy was reading an article about a hippy child who was now setting up a cabin in his own parent's backyard and trafficking in illicit drugs. 'I'he parents of the hippy child were cowering behind the curtains of their home peering out at the "happenings" in their back yard. One trembling parent said to the other one:

"Do you think that we dare in some way or another, tell him how we feel about this?"

Now Thecla McCarthy who is the mother of a growing and energetic group of teenagers couldn't believe her eyes at this dialogue. She said to me:

"If a parent can't tell their own children what is good and what is bad - - what kind of chaos is this?"

She had no more time to discuss the subject however, for she was readying her two teen-age sons to get off on their summer adventure working on a haying ranch in Oklahoma and she had just finished putting her newly-risen bread into the oven as the Texas dewberry jelly bubbled noisily from the range.

Yes, Mam. People of large families live in a world of notoriety all of their own. Invariably they can expect the questions by the interrogating visitor to be of the same brand. "CAN YOU REMEMBER ALL OF THEIR NAMES?" Lori Bertis - when she was 12 years old and the second oldest of a family of eleven children heard this critical question by a visitor to their home. A woman said to her mother Lynn Bertis, "Can you remember all their names?" Lori herself answered the visitor's question with:

"Oh, my mother can remember all of our names alright. IT'S OUR GODPARENTS' NAMES THAT SHE GETS MIXED UP ON!!"

If it is true that: "children have to identify with someone in order to be themselves." Why do they run away from home? To get away from the someone whom they think that they are?

There are real problems however. My neighbor in Texas and I couldn't get our fourteen-agers to go anywhere. Even school was a drag. "That dumb school, that kooky teacher, those bratty kids, those creepy boys, etc." My neighbor with only one child left me musing: 'That fortunate child. Mother and daughter have the opportunity and the "time" to go places together - - to do detailed things together. I conjectured that there should be no end of companionship; of prenatal and parental attentions."

But the beleaguered mother wailed: "I can't get Patti to go anywhere or to do anything. She doesn't even want to go to the same church that I do. When she goes somewhere finally, I ask her what she did or said. She says: "nothing."

I told my all-Texan neighbor:

"I can sympathize with you. I have one child people just her age and it gives you such a nullified feeling after all of these years of nurturing." I offered my sympathy.

"Guess what" my neighbor said. "Patti is just dying to go to a dance tonight at Allen Military Academy!" Do you think that you could talk Irene into going with her?" We both agreed that there was no harm in trying.

••• A short while later I passed the two fourteen-agers under discussion and as I stood in the doorway of their bedroom. I became the unsuspecting audience of this memorable conversation:

Patti: "Mom thinks that I'm going to that stupid Military Academy dance tonight. She thinks that you might like to go too. Boy! Is it ever icky icky ugh! Those creepy boys, they come up to the car to escort you to the ball - all stiffened up.

Mom says: 'Look at those darling little boys, all dressed up in those adorable uniforms!' It's all so icky, icky-- besides, none of them can dance. Mom told me that either I go to the dance or I go nowhere!

Irene: "Let's go nowhere!

"We can have a lot of fun!"

'The tail end of this highly-charged family

episode was that my unsuspecting husband took both teenagers bowling that night. And in my mind's dialogue the words of the Ancient Mariner resounded through my fears.

"Whatever you do or say to children---you must be consistent!"
When I was a lass at fourteen, Dear Old Dad said to/ me:

"Lancashire Lass!! Madame Plabalablah do something!
In the name of the King, - go someplace and do something! Read a good book !! Don't mill around. GET GOING! Be fearful! I The Irish keep their pigs under the kitchen stove!"

But even when Dear Old Dad died - - I \vas to all appearances standing and milling about. I stayed to hear if his last words would be: "All Ashore That's Going Ashore." Instead he said to the lady standing next to me: "I don't want to leave you, Sally." He looked at me and said: "I thought that you had to work today." I replied: "I heard that you were dying so I just came to say goodbye." Johnny I knew had nothing to fear from His questioning Creator for it was widely known that Johnny would give anyone "the shirt off of his back." H e was also known as a soft touch for money borrowers and as Walter Bryan put it so aptly in The Improbable Irish:

"That even in the worst days of the Famine itself, when people were dying by the thousands, the poor Irish never refused admission to the poorest and most abject mendicant."

Of himself, Johnny always remarked: "I have only one suit. Some people have ten suits. You can only wear one suit at a time!" That's what he learned in his hey days in Liverpool. He rarely, if ever, took second helpings of a meal - - saying cautiously while wafting his hand in a dramatic motion at the second helping while with the other hand he patted his chest:
"ENOUGH IS AS GOOD AS A FEAST! A MEAL FIT FOR A KING!"

Dear Old Dad's brother Albert, raised in the same family, would take an extremely large first helping berating those people who took small firsts and then small seconds. When the meal was over he asked to see the pan that the puddin' was made in saying: "May as well finish it all off--don't want to see anything go to waste!

Anne Holmes, a nurse friend of ours attached herself it us as though we had something interesting to say! For some reason every time she went out of our door she would shout:

"DON'T THROW THE BABY OUT WITH THE BATHWATER! It is sorry to think of the baby going out with the bath water. Her husband, who built golf courses, always preached: The poor have to pull themselves up by their boot straps!" (Boots? Straps?)

One fine day, after we prayed the rosary at a funeral home, Anne looked up at my husband to earnestly say, "I wish you were my parents!" She was five years older than us and she knew the problems we were having with some of our children. One day she questioned her father rather bluntly: 'Why were there only two of us?"

My podiatrist remarked that his only daughter was glad that she had no brothers or sisters, that way she will get "a bigger piece of the pie."
Some people are still angry with their parents. One girl who was one of fifteen children had to do a lot of ironing. She is still talking about it. The lady who lived across from us was peeved with her parents. She was an only child. "My parents never talked to me and my father used to take my cousins fishing and left me at home."

You can't have it both ways is a saying that I

never understood.

Dear Old Dad always said: "Keep it down to a College Roar!"
Gird up your Loins
St. Polycarp pray for us.

Chapter five
Pardon Our Human Love

Many people fear quoting other people out of context. This can very subtly be done. But when we quote a dogmatic conclusion there is usually no problem. In 1964 a Belgian couple visited Canada, they were matrimonial counsellors. They observed that "North American women are in danger of losing their femininity. In fact, some of them have already gone too far in trying to eclipse their husbands as heads of families. Now this philosophy, or more correctly said, this observation, meets head on with the concepts of Betty Freidan who is an organizer of the .women's Lib movement and authoress of The Feminine Mystique." (Which I think should have been titled: "The .Feminine Mistake.")"

For Betty, every woman must have a career in order to find herself and in order to find happiness. She feels deeply that women have "sacrificed the right to honorable contribution" by not making life plans" geared to their real abilities." Betty feels that a woman can only realize her femininity and her "identity only in work that . . is of real value to society--work for which society usually pays.

I think that we all get the message that Mrs. Fretdan is trying to convey to us. A lot of mothers have complained about feeling like a "hired helper." The profession at home has the common label of "the housewives trap." Its very name does not give one the feeling of a personal freedom.

Erma Bombeck, noted columnist, said that before she wrote her famous column, she took out her hostilities by "rolling up into a fetal position and humming." That beat whiskey and hot fudge sundaes,

We have here two conflicting views. The Belgian counsellor,Mrs. Gaston Falisse said that the female should play the role of a participant with her husband but with the realization that she is dependant upon him. "I don't like to see a woman trying to battle with her husband in order to obtain .freedoms which she· does not really need. This just makes her less feminine and more superior to her husband in attitude. It is very important for the sake of the children, if there are any, that a harmonious balance is maintained between the two partners in the marriage."

Of course, if a woman has a full time career, the children won't notice any conflict of ideas because they won't be around their parents, as the Feminists are pushing for professionally run nurseries. (So that even the women running the nurseries will be career minded women, doing work for which society pays well.)

So we have planted here two different worlds of thought. I wonder if there is such a thing as a compromise?

Arguments in our house are not in absentee. Here is a recent conversation my husband and I had:

"Are you still rearranging your words?" innocently and quietly asked the sleepy professor, feeling the lateness of the night clamour over him. My answer was a challenging defensive.

"Words?"
"Sentences then." he compromised.
(I recalled what I had read that Samuel Beckett said:

"Every word is like an unnecessary stain on silence and nothingness." · The plays get pretty absurd then; like a play composed entirely of sighs!)

"Yes, yes," I bragged. "I'm busily putting one sentence after the other and some sentences before the other. What can it be? A purging of the self? A therapeutic deal, no doubt." Said the professor who was slipping away slowly into the sleep of the innocent.

My Irish quickened to measure up to his Bohemian curiosity. "It's certainly not as conscientious about words as you philosophers are.. Do you remember the other night when a group of you philosophers were giving your individual opinions on which movies were obscene and which ones were not? Well, there is no problem as to the answers as Webster has the answer for you!: Obscene: lewd, foul, indecent, coarse, smutty, dirty, impure, etc. So on this basis, all of the movies were obscene."

He yawned. I gazed at his fillings. "Now you have to analyze the words lewd, foul, indecent, coarse, smutty, dirty, impure, etc…zzzzzzzzzzz. This string of z's is concrete evidence that the philosopher was sleeping and his philosophy book fell into my neck.

You can't hit your husband when he is sleeping! All the innocence of their youth shines through the rigamortis of the day and you say that you would marry them all over again. You can always burn their toast in the morning, or mis-match their socks.

As the book lie open beneath my eyes I read and heard Socrates say: "I mean when they told you that you must be careful not to let me deceive you----the implication being that I am a skillful speaker. I thought that it was peculiarly brazen of them to tell you this without a blush, since they must know that they will soon be effectively confuted when it becomes obvious that I have not the slightest skill as a speaker- - - - - - - unless, of course, by a skilful speaker they mean one speaks the truth."

As I too was dragged by sleep into the subconscious life - - I heard the uneven whispers of snoring which were a living tribute to the love of truth itself.

I can always cook his eggs like rocks in the morning!

I feel close to professors and some of them love me. An English Literature professor told me not to show my "words" to anyone lest we all get hung up on a semi-colon and...pfftt! no written book. "A very intelligent remark" coaxed my spouse. Professors are dear to me. They wear old clothing usually, and appreciate the simpler things in life like laughter and the need of it.

One reason babies are so content is because they do not have the task of finding a title for a doctoral thesis! Many lay people do not realize that if, and when, you are half way through writing your thesis, and then you discover quite accidentally that someone else has beaten you to your precise original theme! You must start all over again!! It doesn't matter what the topic is but you do have to have an ORIGINAL. As we can see this is a very mean cause for many earnest profs.

What professor has the time to hang around to prove an invisible existence to a chubby little or chubby big kid? Both college professors and housewives, have much more important ideas to prove. They have papers to read, diapers to wash, papers to write, papers to edit, papers to type, floors to clean, papers to dream about writing, dogs to put outside, papers· to analyze, and babies to change. They all have their identities to discover and their husbands or wives to keep. They also must be very careful not to get the diaper liners mixed up with the student's written theses!!

Another family argument was brewing in the Irish stew. It didn't upset the children because the children were busy arguing over a box of crayons.

"What if I ever did become a College President one day?" mused the Philosopher-King. What in the world would I do with you? You know that you must develop some tact, some poise, and some diplomacy to hang around with us profs. I know some people who get stoned three sheets to the wind and never say the things that you say, stone cold sober!"

"You can always borrow a friend when it comes time to ·entertain guests because I don't see any instant change in my built-in prenatal system of saying the right thing at the wrong time." I muttered miserably.

"You've been hanging around the kids too long," he surmised. "I need to take you out someplace." Instantly my suspicious nature came to the surface. Some people call it a form of paranoia.

I said: "Last week I wanted to see the site where

the Mexicans, Indians, and the Texans battled it out, and you said that you wouldn't care to see a historic site where a bunch of people died." He walked away muttering "horrible thought!" unaware of the fact that two little people had attached themselves to his shoulder and another one had tied a dog leash a round his leg.

Everyday at 11:30 all over America kindergartener's trot in from school and they basically and implicitly know that there is nothing in the world that you would love to hear about more than their Kindergarten repertoire:

"Mom! Where are you? Do you know where to buy balloons, Mom? Angilise said that only her mommy and daddy know where to buy balloons. I let Carl Pooska color in my coloring book. I let Karen take my coloring book home with her. . She promised me that she wouldn't go out of the lines.

Helen said to me: "Go away Jeanne. I don't like you!" That's what she said and I didn't do nothing! We were just walking along and-----WOWIE!!!! Mom! Is Helen ever little! She's only as small as a three-year old!" When Jeanne was in her early teens, she surprised herself one day and she spoke optimistically!

"I didn't know I was going to feel so good today!"

Over twenty years I have learned that many a kindergartener's heart has been found broken amongst a bag of balloons and that many a tear has been shed.

About Monsters we learn from our four-ager. I asked Madeline this morning why our baby is so afraid of the dark? "She thinks that there is a monster in there!" She almost convinced me so· I asked: "How do yon know that there is such a thing as a monster?"

"Oh, there is a monster house and the monster lives there in his monster house" she instructed me as though she had been schooled in monster theory. I forced the issue: "Did you ever see a monster--- really??" "No, but he might come someday!" This sounded like a final warning to me. That's what I deserve for hanging around four-agers.

When Madeline was a three-ager she was looking out of the window at the house next door. Finally she said: "Is our house outside too?"

She heard about a little three-ager boy being killed by a car, on the radio. She said: "Where did they bury their dead little boy? Can his mamma look down into the hole to see him? Does she cry when she sees in? I don't wanna' go to heaven, Mom, I like it right here in my house!" One main advantage about hanging around with the younger set is that you don't have an opportunity to lose your tact, poise or diplomacy. They keep you busy thinking!

As a housewife and mother and a wishful alcoholic I ·found the only place in Bryan, College Station, Texas for me where I could find some booze at a parish cocktail party. All that we do at a cocktail party is Talk. Talk. Talk. It would put a tape recorder to shame. So the only thing else to do is---drink. I was hoping to get in on some interesting conversations, something a little above the peanut-butter and jelly crowd when a certain professor found out via the wine-vine that my husband and I had ten children. (You know, those little darlings that think a plunger is for bouncing around the house on.) Oh, boy. One night out a month for me and he had to come along to talk shop. I got his message over a whiskey sour that eased the pain:

"I have finally found a thesis title which no other human brain has devised. Not even in their weakest moments. The title of it is, Some Immediate Effects of a Smoking Environment on Children of Elementary School Age. The purpose of it is to determine the immediate effects of a cigarette smoking environment on children of elementary school age. Special emphasis is going to be made to determine the extent to which a cigarette smoking environment affects the nonsmoking child's heart rate, systolic and diastolic blood pressure and the amount of carbon monoxide in the blood. In addition, an effort is being made to determine whether smoking homes or non-smoking homes are involved and if the male subjects are affected differently than the female subjects.

Completely unnerved I replied with my usual loss of diplomacy: "That calls for a good stiff drink, or a drink for a good stiff." I loved to joke and always prided myself on my existing sense of humor. But remembering the effect of my humor on others and my husband's various admonitions about my lack of tact - - I drank and stood with glass raised safely to my lips. No one ever bothered to talk to me at a party so much before so I know that there was a method to his foolishness. He took a drink and continued:

"I would like to borrow your children to prove my thesis title with." (A diplomacy even I had not thought of.)

The whiskey sours were tickling my imagination. Could he possibly mean those monsters whom I have hidden at home harboring all of those rampant free wills?? My subconscious brought forth the ·. voice of my fourteen-ager:

"What? If you THINK THAT T AM GOING TO SOME CRAZY LABORATORY WITH SOME KOOKY PROF FOR AN INSANE EXPERIMENT WITH SOME FOOLS BLOWING SMOKE IN MY FACE AND A NURSE PUMPING MY BLOOD ALONG WITH THOSE NUTTY, PUNKY KIDS OF YOURS ****You have got to be kidding!"

My husband hudged his way over to us while jiggling his little free ice cubes. He had heard our conversation and he spoke with tact:

"IF YOU CAN CATCH 'EM. YOU CAN HAVE 'EM!"

The smoking professor laughed and I relaxed for the first time that evening: He said, "Ha, ha, ha, ha, ha - - that's what everybody says." He admitted that he had five available victims of his own. "My wife is a nurse and she will be over to get your children in a few weeks. We'll give them twenty-five cents for a milk shake." My tact slipped again, oops! "I figured that your wife was a professor or a nurse. Everyone's wife is. Well, you can't buy a milkshake for twenty-five cents anymore - - -"I had wasted my poise and grace for he was gone - - - enveloped in a cloud of smoke!

My evening had flown with time and the day for the experiment had come and had gone. David, our 12-ager, was delirious. "What delicious fun! I got to shout into the tube - - third cigarette! And I got to tie the rubber hoses around Mary and Andrea's arms while they watched cartoons about people smoking!"

My ten-ager Mary Elizabeth did not fare as well. She came home in tears with a very sore arm which had barely survived two shots.

If stomping one's feet and banging on one's wall is poise—I had it and I vowed that that would be the last time I would help a college professor with his thesis! "Oh, but Mom, come on! ·It might be a fun thing!" moaned David.

One of my sorest hang-ups is squirt guns and they had given the sweet little children the empty shot needles. They make great squirt guns! (Maybe to put out cigarettes with?)

I said to David. "Why do you talk more than the girls?"

"Because there are eight of them and only one of me!" came the undebatable twelve---ager logic. At this time a four-ager appeared on the scene of life Madeline.

Madeline said: "Hey. I don't wanna' go back into that bedroom because there is an elephant and a lion in there!" We looked unperturbed. "And didn't the lion bite you?" we said. She looked at us with that irreplaceable four-ager look of disgust and superiority: "Bite me? When it is just a teeny little lion way over on a teeny little dresser? Jump down from the dresser, when it **is** asleep?" I said: "Oh, and what about the elephant, is he little too?" The child sighed. She sized apart her small plump hands--giving one the idea of the size of the elephant. "Hmmmmnnn--just a little baby elephant" I said.

The prof-at-home-admidst-it-all was finishing his breakfast. He looked concerned enough. "Has she been drinking cough syrup?" he wondered.

I tried to sound convincing. "Nah" All four-agers dig like that--why just the other day Madeline asked:
"Can a bear eat a leopard?

"Can a leopard eat a bear?"

Dear Old Dad always sang:
"If you're from DIXIE
If you're from DIXIE
Then I'm from DIXIE too!"
Gird up your loins
St. Polycarp, Pray for us!

Andrea's wedding day

Jeannes wedding

Five grandchildren enjoying ice cream

My daughter Mary with her daughter Shannon and her newborn James Ian

David...five years old and a future Texan

Dad and David watching Nicole's graduation

Terese and her daughter Nicole

Rick...all dressed up

Difficulties can be resolved by the Holy Rosary

Father John doubted that Pinocchio had made a full and truthful confession.

Father John

Are They All Yours?

Maddie and Andrea riding their horse in Washington

Andrea, age 9, eating lunch

Irene (2 years old) with Dear Old Dad

Bobbie and Madeline taking a picture

My husband Richard and I

Finis Elijah, deceased at 22

Maddie with her happy self

Madeline, laughing at her childhood wisdom

Bobbie Sue at 11

Ann with her children (top left: Stan, Zoe, nephew David, Serena, and Tonya)

Are They All Yours?

Ann, 29 years old, became a Registered Nurse

My daughter Irene

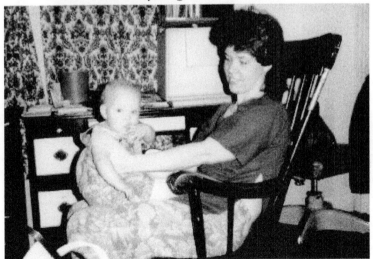

Andrea with her daughter Rachel

Chapter Six
And Madeline Said:

Most adults would like to learn all that they can about teenagers, but they remember that their own teenage was too traumatic for them. This makes it impossible to go back into their own teenage to analyze their children. A lot of people have said that they do not like to think about their childhood. Some adults and orators have called the young adult a "teen-age monster" while other people think that the three-ager time is the monster age.

Sometimes the young adults have the tendency to emulate the gangster idols of old. College students at Yale had their "Bogey" week--- showing full length movies of Humphrey Bogart for a week. It became the fad to stop in the halls with choice lines, one of them being:

"I don't have to show you no stinkin' badge!" Young adulthood is the time of mystery and probably could be the most interesting time of our lives. There certainly is no end to their questions and everything of the day seems traumatic to them.

Questions such as:
"What kind of bread am I eating?"
"What is this octopus doing in the refrigerator?"
"Where did you get all these kids?"
"Where is my red sweater?"
"Purple ribbon?"
"Lost earring?"
"Did I get a letter?"
"They are your kids, not mine. But I am mine."

The age of mystery. My fourteen-ager washed her long dark brown hair and put it up into huge round rollers made from wrapping paper rolls covered with contact paper. She left them in for a short while then took them out and proceeded to brush her hair straight. "Why bother curling it?" I asked with adult slow-wittedness. "You can't get it to go straight unless you curl it first." "Gee, you're old-fashioned, Mom. I'll bet anything that you still use those soggy old-fashioned tea bags!" I secretly wondered when they were going to stop talking like gangsters and to also stop chewing gum like gangsters.

"Hey, Mom! Will ya' get those brats of yours out of our room! Mom! We're tryin' to have some privacy!"

Mom: "Well, if you have to have so much privacy, how come then it is so noisy?"

Their closets reflect their status in the family. Stuffed with clothes. There is no room for their coats and they "never have anything to wear." They never wear skirts or dresses unless someone else has set the pace. I thought they were going digging the other night. Sloppy jeans, long plaid shorts, straight hair. "Where are you going?" I asked with suspicion. "We're going dancing!" was the casual (too) reply. Well, I thought to myself, I won't have to worry about any boys falling in love with them anyway.

Unless us oldsters can grow to understand the primitive needs of the young adult heart, all their lives will look like a circus to us, as ours does to them.

I had a vacuous mind when I started to bring human babies into the world. I actually asked a person: "When are you supposed to spank them?" I asked the wrong people. They never took the time to analyze when to spank. They were always swinging. A more honest and intellectual friend of mine, Adora Higgins, went to the library and asked for a book on How to Play With Baby. In those early days, Dr. Spock was everyone's friend and savior. Benjamin Spock was the only adult human who had ever learned anything practical about children, so it seemed. He wrote that it was "o.k." if we spanked our offsprings now and then; he explained that they would not hate us forever for it and---best of all we would cool our brain off to leave room for future thoughts.

Early to bed and early to rise
Makes Mama feel rested and ready—for any surprise.

There is no bedtime fussing at our house. By nine o'clock I am so pooped out that I go along quite docilely led by the hand by my three, four, and six-agers. Early to bed! I told the six-ager not to tell me anymore Snow White stories. It was not at all a realistic story about seven little men and one young lady all livening in one little house. I promised them in return that I would read the Five Little Peppers and How They Grew, (Almost as hectic as the house that Jack built).
The four of us snuggled close together in a large double bed all vieing to look at the pictures in the book. I breathed a sigh of relaxation and started to read:

"For times were always hard with them nowadays. Since the father had died, when Phronsie was a baby, Mrs. Pepper had had hard work to scrape together money enough to put bread into the childrens' mouths and to pay the rent of the little brown house."

I was not relaxed anymore. To be sure, Mrs. Pepper "had a stout heart and a cheery face" and the children were very eager to help their mother; it was a desire that grew so great so as to absorb all lesser desires.

Our six-ager Jeanne, started to worry about their baby.
"Where's the baby now?"
"What is the baby eating?"
"Does the baby have a warm bed?" "Why doesn't Polly get an outside baby sitting job?"
I tossed the book into the "unloved heap" of reading material. "I'll sing to you", offered the three-ager Madeline with the stout heart:
"Ohhhh, do you know the muffin man, the muffin man?
The muffin man?—1,2,3,4,5,6,7,8,9,10. It pays to have your children put you to sleep.

Housewives, as such, are not the low man on the

totem pole of everyone. Some people actually pay money and run advertisements with the hopes of obtaining a housewife! In Alabama in 1962, the local Cullman newspaper ran this advertisement:

"Man, age 28, wants a wife.
Has lived alone since 8 years old!
Have all the food and furniture
That you will need. Call me at this number."

(I don't remember the classification. It was either Business Opportunity or Miscellaneous Wanted).

Our three-ager daughter Madeline turned four-ager today. Last week she began to be filled with great expectations! "What is my name going to be?" she clapped with eager anticipation. What is my name going to be?"

When the great day came she glanced down at her lack of growth during the night and she was very disgusted with herself. "Oh, yeah," she said with contempt. "Little kids are four years old!"

One day when we had a borrowed TV, she was watching Captain Kangaroo as she ate her morning eggs. The program changed while she was watching it. She was not aware of the change. As I came back into the room I said: "Oh, you are watching

Lucy!" "Is that who that is?" she pondered. "I thought that was dancing bear's mother!"

This same little cherub is a real dragnet in a supermarket! She sits in her place of honor squarely at the back of the shopping cart, facing her smaller sister's back—who is sitting with her feet dangling out of the front by the handle.

Madeline breaks the silence of people's thinking with a question: "Do dead people have their eyes closed?" "Hmmm, yes, " I replied taking .49 times three and a half pounds. "THEN, HOW COME THAT DEAD FISHES HAVE THEIR EYES OPEN?" she screamed with lady fair rancor. I turned my head from the hamburger only to be stared back at by all those bulging eyeballs of the dead mackerals lying side by side. I thought to myself: "Hmmmm, they probably have no eyelids and someone has written a good master's thesis on that." I figured that I had to watch myself; this kid was going to get her sex education in the supermarket! Now she was singing at the top of her larynx: "John's brown body lies a'moulding in the grave!" I bought her a bright blue giant-sized jaw breaker, which are aptly named (hoping to fill the void). Secretly I hate jaw-breaker producers. I'm convinced that they never had any children of their own.

After five minutes of trying to get the giant ball into her mouth and only managing to get the bright blue all over her face and hands—she sadly handed the-then-very-slimy-ball back to me. "Won't fit" she moaned pensively. I quickly put it into my purse. It was better than dropping it amongst the apples!

By then Madeline was shouting loudly and pointing to a new baby lying in a supermarket cart.

"Wow! Is that a newborn baby?
Is that a born baby?
Is that a really baby?
Where did they get it?
Does it have any teeth?
Where is the daddy?
What is it doing in that basket? Huh?
Did they buy it here?"

One thing she was sure of, and that is that all babies have mothers AND fathers, for she said: "Where is the Daddy?" But what they forget is that mother and father are the ones who brought the baby into the world.

What usually looks like an uneventful day at our house usually turns to trauma.

"What color are rabbits?" There sat Madeline poised with crayon in hand. There was no time to delay answers. I had a gnawing ache in my heart that she knew what color rabbits were as she had been analyzing them very closely at the Texas A & M Agricultural Experimental grounds every Sunday on our week-end excursion. Another traumatic day I had lied to her by telling her that swans were "yellow" simply because I rationalized that she did not have any white crayons and I did not want to start a grand search or a grand exodus up to the corner store.

"There is no such thing as "yellow swans!" came the livid reply, and said in such earnest with her built-in-prenatal wisdom of a three-ager. "Errr, well, sometimes they get dirty and then they look yellow!" I adlibbed and tried to look into her honest steady gaze.

In the Houston Post I read about a college professor, whom I think would rather remain autonomous and anonymous. He wrote his doctoral thesis on the "Age-Year Nine." The theme of his thesis ran as follows:

"after nine year old, shopping at the store is just another chore to do for the irritable old Mom. Before nine lies the crucial stage where we are most interested in prices and trademarks and we have the will to shop!"

The age of nine holds a magical coincidences of decision to him. In order to learn something about the children of whom he was writing his thesis, he said:

"You won't believe this, but I actually got down on my knees and played blocks with a group of four-year olds, to learn more about what they might be thinking." (HOUSTON POST, 1969)

If we could read into the thoughts of those four-agers they might be saying something like this:

"Hmmm, what does this big guy want??
Cus, no big guys play with blocks.
Hey, there's a bug on his pants.
One of those 'tater bugs. It won't hurt him.
Daddy says that big men built the Empire State Building!
So, this guy must be looking for his keys, maybe."

They may have been thinking that he looks just

like Uncle Charlie; or that maybe his tie is red just like their new finger paints' red. Or this economist from the University of Texas might hear:

"If you are looking for Mom---she is in the kitchen."

One cautious sounding day, Madeline Herrity, now a big four-ager, was smiling at me with a secret smile coming surely came from the treasured corners of her little heart. "She loves me", I thought securely. "Will she tell me her secret?" Her blonde hair, blue eyes, and small pointed white teeth belied her words dripping with unintentional sadism:

"I know who you are talking to again! Yourself!" I lied brilliantly again. "I am not talking to myself. I am singing!" While bursting with pride of my afterthought I heard her say: "When is Dad going to take me to that Mrs. Robinson movie which he promised me---NEVER?"

Mother is the seeded-core of the hard-core society. She can't be replaced. Not even a test-tube could:

Have all the time in the world to find the other sock. Doctor measles and more measles, mumps, flu, pink-eye. Scissor wounds, take arms out of wringers, rescue contact lenses from the drain.

Fight infections, stys in many eyes, broken teeth, pimples. Write letters to their Bishops about the TRUTH! We mothers save our loveliest repressed smile for the inevitable remark when we've been invited to visit:

"OH, BY THE WAY! I FORGOT TO TELL YOU BEFORE YOU CAME—THAT ALL OF MY CHILDREN HAVE A STRANGE VIRUS INFECTION. I HOPE YOUR CHILDREN DON'T GET IT!" hahahahahahahahahaha

In the 1990's divorce was the topic of the day. A lady professor with her husband had a PHD. She travelled a lot for her job with Texas A&M. One fine day she discovered that most of her colleagues were divorced or getting a divorce. She said: "So I quit to stay home and cook for my husband and children!"

Another professor in education at A&M went to a conference with colleagues and found out that everyone at the table was divorced.

A cousin of mine who, with her husband and children, came to the states from Liverpool, England obtained a divorce because "we were alike as CHALK and CHEESE!"

My husband was seeing the divorce in his

department. He said to me: "If you leave home, I will take your pictures of Jesus and your crucifix. But I'm not worried about you. You're not friendly!"

Dear Old Dad always said: "Hang on to your hats!"
Gird up your Loins!
St. Polycarp pray for us.

Chapter Seven
The Art of Saying "No"

We come upon another seemingly calm day in our household; the trauma that lie within was obscured behind a song on the blaring radio:

"If you oooonly loved me half as much as I love you". It was breakfast time. Just a seemingly calm and ordinary and undesirable enough Day. I would have to open my big mouth: As I poured my husband's coffee:

"I wonder what it would HAVE BEEN like if we had had only two children instead of TEN!" (The famous Dr. Lieberman had said that two children are company and that three children are a crowd. "Children from larger families are less self-reliant—and less mature than children from small families", he said!)

Heaving fourth a sigh as though it came from a middle of a dream—my husband replied:

"Pass the sugar please. Our first two children

are gone from home now—and we would just be fighting." This remark wetted my curiosity:

"What would we be fighting about?? After all, I love you MORE than you love me!" My husband philosophized through the coffee grounds: "You don't love me HALF as much as I love YOU!" As I had been on my feet for a few minutes I could shout louder than he could: "I love you—MORE THAN you love me!!"

Our adventurous and someday horsewoman nine-year old daughter and seventh child, Andrea Louise changed our trend of thought by asking: "Pardon me, are you finished with your coffee cups yet?? I'm ready to clean off the table now". She put the broom away and started to sing huskily:

"They shall knowww we are Christians by our love, by our love------- they shall knowww we are Christians by our love!"

After she busily cleaned the table, she promptly asked this question:

"Mom? Can I clean the bird cage now?"

This innocent enough sounding question was to

bring forth from me that scream of self defense that usually billows forth when changes ensue which I am not prepared for. "No! You may not clean the birdcage!" (My feeling of emotions brought thoughts of a past Thanksgiving day. As I was meditating on the taste of my wild rice dressing, I saw children carrying dressers down a hallway. Upon inquiring, I was informed that they were changing bedrooms!)

Meanwhile, Andrea was sizing up the situation and she said: (With anguish) "Oh, dear, the poor, poor dirty bird. Hasn't been cleaned in a hundred years!

Probably get sick". As I sized up the predicament and especially the look on Andrea's face, "Oh! OK. Clean the birdcage."

"No! No!" These were the emphatic cries of a two-ager as she kicked and struggled to avoid having her shoes put on. I tickled her. "Kootchie, kootchie, kooooo!" Ouch! My finger! A struggle ensued. The age old struggle of putting shoes on a two-ager. I got the shoes on! A look of triumph was mine. I outwitted the two-ager!...Ten minutes later, Bobbi-Sue got the shoes off! I sought after the Philosopher. Surely Plato or Aristotle had a few words in Greek, words of wisdom, which could apply to two-agers. "What do ya' do with two-agers when you want to put shoes on them?" I found the philosopher searching for a clean shirt in a large closet.

The cry from the bowels of the closet floor slapped me like a wet towel: "YA' PUT 'EM 'TA WORK!"

There was no time to translate from the Greek, but it was Greek to me and in the oncoming years I deciphered the phrase to apply to the mother, and not to the baby.

The day will come soon when the two-ager will be a fourteen-ager and with all the other fourteen-agers across America, their spirits will suffer. Their real voices will resound bemoaningly:

"Mom! My ends are split (the existential cry!)
"Mom! My pants are too loose!
"Mom! The boys at school threw a dirty old mustard sandwich all over my desk!
"Mom! I can't sing! Someone stole my comb!
"Mom! I got a 50 on my Science Test. That dumb teacher.
"Mom! Got anything gooood to eat??"

As I was going through my morning chores of

cleaning the bedrooms, I listened to the daily news broadcast from San Antonio. The news announcer reported that even grade school children were now sniffing glue and that sixth graders were now smoking pot. I looked in my newspaper clippings and reread the article that Louis Hutchinson wrote about working mothers. It read: "In March, 1965 nearly 26 million women were in the civilian labor force.....Last October there were 28.5 million women in the labor force, an increase of 1.2 per cent over October of 1965. At that rate, we'll exceed the 30 million figure by 1970."

The announcer on the radio went on to say that the juvenile delinquency age is now from ten years to eighteen years. "What is next?" He concluded his report to the unseen audiences. Next week on the same news broadcast---three eleven-agers (boys) raped a ten-ager girl in a locked broom closet while her teacher tried to get the door open.

   The fourteen-ager said: "Mom is this skirt too short?"
Mom said: "The answer is YES."
Fourteen-ager: "Well, I don't care! I don't care what Sister Carmel says, I'm going to wear it anyway!"

The four year old said: "Mom, do I have to eat my egg?"

Mom said: "Yes."

A clenched jaw replied: "No! I'm not gonna!!"

A President of a Catholic College said: "A person has the right to dissent, only then can he truly affirm."

When does this right began to take on Reality?

What Will Happen to Father's Mind?

He may change his ideas about children having the right to dissent before they affirm. He may set a definite age-limit, if for no better reason than to keep from going insane. The sheer logical reasoning of self-preservation.

One evening I found myself standing next to a not-very-old college professor who in turn was standing next to a young college professor. Both philosophers. The older one of the two said:

"Wow! I came home from work today, all tired out and guess what happened? My four year old son came up to me and said to me:

"Dad, may I go to see the movie, Candy?" The young philosopher who did not have to grapple with such weighty problems as this said: "Gee whiz, what do you say when they start asking questions like that?" The tired professor growled: "I kicked him in his Adam's apple!"

Under the Criminal Code of Canada, it is an offense to print, publish, distribute, or circulate any obscene written matter and the Crown Prosecutor said that the book Candy's contents were "obscene written matter." The nineteen-year old girl, who was in the movie, said: "I think that it is a very funny picture. I'm glad that I did it. It says something. It is the world that is dirty." The interviewer in the article asked of her another question:

"What do your parents have to say about your prancing about in the near-nude on the screen?" The girl answered: "I often ask their opinion. I often take their advice. But not this time. Parents have no right to tell a child to do this or to do that!"

If her parents have no right to tell her to do this or to do that; then it is not logical for her to ever ask their advice, for they have no rights. (The American newspaper said that: "the movie Candy was the ultimate dirty movie.")

A bit of Tom-Foolery

The Indians had a word for no! It was heap no! Big-Chief-Sit-Um-On-The-Fire-And-Put-Em-Out, said: "Do you think that I am going to let you handsome young warrior with the small flap to romp through the Bluebonnets after dark with the beautiful Minne-ha-ha in her mini-ha-ha skirt? Ha! What you think that I am? Big-Chief-Old-Fool-Like-An-Old-Fool? First you run through long lone line of ---hatchets!"

My six-teen-ager said to me as I stirred my Irish Stew: "Mom, come on, I want you to come with me when I buy my bathing suit." Staring closely at the carrots and potatoes, I said: Do you mean that I have a choice of bathing suits?" This, I thought, put me in a position of decision. "Oh, no, I have the suit all picked out. I just want you to see it," was the teenage-logic, with grace.

I stood there in the dressing room of the Department store, feeling quite naked in my pre-natal built-in wisdom with the saleslady's head head popping in and out of the curtain, saying as she popped: "Doing O.K. in here? Doing O.K.?" I put on my sunglasses. I said: "Not much there—is there?" "You are just not used to it. They are all pretty much like that." She popped out again. I weakly, and without courage, reassured Teri (to the tune of twenty dollars) that she could always put a lima bean in her navel.

...The following day when we were swimming at Summerville Lake, my daughter Teri-s suit looked very conservative to me and I saw the rule of fashion she was up against. The Tremendous Great Society's democracy. I hardly noticed her yawning navel; I was glad that she wasn't falling out of her bra. One of the teenagers there (seventeen-ish) was running around in a pink-bottom-ruffled bikini with a pink-ruffled piece of cloth on the top which dipped low in the front. She was romping and cavorting like a goat animal which had no other care in the world.

You can't blame some common-ordinary housewives and mothers to run scared when even Presidents of Universities have baby-sitting problems these days. The students of some large Catholic Universities have conned the Jesuits into having parental (parietal) hours. The administrators did not want to say "yes". They had to. They rationalized: "they are lowering the voting age to 18.

If we can give them the responsibility of voting---certainly we can give them the responsibility of parietal hours". Unquote.

And so they set the scene:
Surrounded by one small bedroom.
One hard chair.
One soft bed.
One cool beer.
Hard lips.
A mid-summer night's dream.
Two small minds.

The President of the university left for safer grounds.

So now the prayer hours of the religious are turned into unpaid baby-sitting hours by the will of the children. And all of this time, Mommy and Daddy thought that Junior and Sis were doing their homework. But then Mommy and Daddy always were stupid! Junior has been working his way through Daddy's money. No one told Mommy and Daddy to go without new underwear just so that the babies could have a college education! In fact, no one asked to be born! What about their Free Will? Didn't you sin against their free will by bringing them into the world when they didn't even ask to be born."

"At our first birth we were born of necessity without our knowledge." Four Witnesses pg 185.

Why are so many people mad at St. Joseph? A priest in Washington said after a mass, "We put St. Joseph in the lobby and not in the church because HE NEVER SAID A WORD!" A parish in Texas got rid of him altogether.

One fine day I was sitting in a church in College Station and I noticed the iron rod that St. Joseph had been hanging on up on the wall—was EMPTY. The maintenance man happened to be standing by. I asked him, "What happened to St. Joseph?" He looked worried and troubled. He motioned for me to come upstairs to the boiler room. Inside he pointed and there stood St. Joseph with paint all dripping down with the lilies pulled out of his hand leaving rust.

The Maintenance man and I carried him to my station wagon never even thinking someone might question us. At home, our daughter Therese, is an artist. She and her friend antiqued him. Anne Holmes took him to her home and carved carpenter tools for his hand. Our two husbands then carried him up the red carpet of the Church and stood him on the right behind the railing that was there. No one thought to take a picture! No cell phones! He looked so handsome!

St. Joseph stood there a number of years! They may have thought someone influential had brought him back. No one seemed to notice us!

When I called years later to question what happened to St. Joseph when he disappeared I received the arrogant reply from a teaching lady: "I've been here for 20 years! St. Joseph has never been here!!" A nun from the hospital said, "I'm glad they took the lilies out of his hands!"

I have heard it said from a very reliable source that we are now regressing from being a Scientific Era into a Philosophical, Metaphysical, and a Theological Era. The Ancient Greeks resorted to Philosophy when they realized that they had started to leave baby girls and deformed and retarded infants, out on the vast lone waste spaces to die of starvation.

The Ancient Greeks started then: to wonder.
To wonder is a philosophical act, defined by Webster as "an event that causes astonishment."
The Greeks speculated then about themselves.
"Who are we?"

"What are we?"
"What are we doing?"
So it must also follow: Where are we?"
And finally the all important:
"How and Why are we?"

   We could always go to Confession to try to find out how and why we are, and who we are.

   It is 2013. Today the confessional has gone out of style. Everyone is their own Pope. Women are using the confessional to nurse their babies in. A Mormon girl said to me: "If one believes in confessions, they will be in the confessional all of their lives". I stayed in the confessional all of my life and I am proud of it! The priest never asked me how many children I had. I was glad of that. I felt guilty already. At mass I miss the old time beating of the chest and shouting: "Mia Culpa! Mia Culpa! Mia Maxima Culpa! I always felt like a new person then.

   A young girl came up to me to say: "We don't have to confess our venial sin anymore." I just heard that you can go to confession online! I was too shocked to answer her. She looked so jubiliant and I was so taken aback, that I wondered where she had gotten that heretical mentality. What should we do with our personal sins? Eat them and swallow them and let them go out in the drain? We have to do something with them. It took a lot of serious thinking. What is left to confess? Everyone is bipolar now—a sort of mental illness. Where can we obtain comfort in absolution?

"Personal sin is no longer revelant in today's historical context." —Father Vincent Miceli S.J.

There is still some confessional business still with some of my friends…..with their made up "Mortal" sins. Pat Farrington would call up to ask: "Is this or that a mortal sin?" (Something ridiculous). I would answer: "No! It is not even a sin!" Pat called Father Steve and he gave her the same answer. The at home Philosopher listened in and said: "Free Counseling!" Then he went back to watching the television.

The famous preacher, Father John O'Connor on his tape, *A Woman Clothed with the Sun*, said to avoid Pariochial schools. You don't get a good catholic education there..

When dear old dad was walking in Johannesburg, Africa, a man came up to him to ask, "Are you Johnny Mapother's son?" When he said yes, the man said, "You walk just like him." A tribute dear old dad kept close to his heart. They both were printers on the ocean liners from Liverpool to New York.

That is why Dear Old Dad always said on his sea worthy legs, "Batten down the hatches!"
Gird up your Loins of understanding
St. Polycarp Pray for Us

Chapter Eight
Humanly Unpremediated Existences

And all this talk brings us to the cold and open reality of humanly unpremeditated existences. At our first birth we were born of a necessity without our knowledge. The only person born into this world, who could choose his own parents, was the divine person: the God man Jesus Christ. It is an open and shut case that not one of us asked to be born. We all know that it would be an impossible feat to ask a child if it would like to be born or not. I mentioned a friend of mine who went right up to her own mother to say, "Why was I born?" The mother did not stop to think sentimentally. She said something that we would call beating around the bush. "Well, you are here now, so make the best of it!"

Our four-year-old daughter, who never stops talking only long enough to think, said to us the other day.

"God is good." I asked her: "How do you know that?" She informed me surely: "Because He made us."

If housewives would catch on once in a while as to their boring existence, they might very well become a vanishing breed. I am getting hard put --- trying to locate any contemporaries.

Now the housewife who lived behind me was a housewife but she does not have the time to "expose" over coffee grounds, which usually turns into a psychiatrist's field day! She waits on her husband hand over foot and if you see a housewife whizzing around the shopping centers that is my housewife friend, Polly Joe Patterson. Now Polly Joe did not ask to be born but she is the friendliest Texan ever brought into the world. All heart and soul and no time for housewifery nonsense! She cleans her house up a barn storm, irons up a mountain of shirts to make them look like a million dollars.

She drives a car like a mechanic and handles her husband's money like an experienced bookkeeper. She does bookkeeping for her husband when he needs one at his office and babysits her grandchildren; having time left over to take all of our kids and hers for baton lessons. You couldn't classify her as a common-ordinary housewife what sits and knits and chases dustballs for a hobby. When the monsoons come in Bryan, and Polly feels a little down - she whips out The Power of Positive Thinking and cleans up after the dog. So there are housewives and then there are housewives.

"Whatcha' doin?" called Polly Jo as she heard the pounding of the typewriter out through the back window on a hot Texas morning.

"Nothing." I told the truth.

"The children told me that you are writing a book," she challenged me trying to scare the cockroaches back into the bushes.

"Well don't get excited," I said. "It's nothing like Alice in Wonderland."

She said, "Thank goodness, and when you write your book please put in some of the bad things-- don't make it all goody-good."

I came out of the back door and wished that she didn't look so sad--and reassured her that I would put in the bad, also. She went home, a friend of mine, sharing my spirit. I received a letter from a friend of mine, and mother of eight growing children who said that her husband would not read any more Christmas letters which always said: "Susie is the star of the Ballerina class; Johnny has his letter in football and all A's on his report; mother just adores her stint as den mother and making cookies for the Girl Scouts, etc." Back at the ranch, it was never like that and it cost a small fortune to start the kids in dancing, football and Girl Scouts.

Everyone is a lot jumpier in these days than they were in Grandma's day. You could always sit and snap beans with Grandma. Take a walk to the mailbox. Quilt in the livingroom (Or just wander around in the pastures trying to catch the mad turkeys. But nowadays, you even have a problem trying to find another housewife. There is one friend of mine though who lives in "going" Los Angeles. She wrote me a letter:

"No one will let me be a housewife; they resent my solitude. They actually disapprove of a woman taking care of her kids and liking it! I love the silence myself! Just give me my kids and a volume of Thoreau and I am happy!
With love,
Marjorie Delaney"

Why begrudge her the peace and the quiet of eleven children? We housewives must never underestimate the importance of our lives. I must tell you this quote of important words of the week by important women of the world) Mrs. Philip Hart, heiress, pilot, anthropology student, and wife of the Michigan senator said:

"Why must we handicap ourselves with the idea that every woman's place is in the kitchen, despite what her talent and capabilities might be?" (Spokesman-Review, Nov. 24, 1969)

That woman is not only rich, she must be mad to think that most of us extra-curricular Americans have the money to do anything else But mix powdered milk in the kitchen and scare up enough grub for a small platoon. It is a fight for me just to keep my rented typewriter out of the Cream of Wheat!

Some friend housewives of mine said, "We feel useless. We never earn any money, all that we do is create. Create bills; create problems. All that we do is spend money. We are beginning to hate money." I reminded them that they also create children. They are re-creators, thereby being recreation for their husbands and - - - lovers in the fullest sense of the term. Most housewives are some of the world's greatest lovers.

That is why we have such a big following. The housewife in her continuous hours of loving earns the money just as fully as does the husband who goes out each morning to "earn his bread in the sweat of his brow." Any husband who thinks that the money is more his because he brings it home - - - or who nags at his wife for buying new shoes for the children --must necessarily trade places with her - - if only for a week.

Housewives, as such, are a vanishing breed. They don't wife the house anymore. Mothers and homemakers??? Yes!! There you can see them (if you look) in all of their beauty. Driving children to class project tours, babysitting, lunch rooms at schools, going to recitals, going to plays. You see the little mothers trying to make a dollar out of fifteen cents at garage sales. You see the little beauty wielding an unwildly supermarket cart overflowing with the basic needs of mankind -- swarmed over at the same time with mankind. You can find her if needs be in her kitchen preparing three meals a day plus twenty snacks, and baking pies that make her old landlord's mouth water. She spends hours sitting in doctors' offices, dentists' offices, optometrists', orthodontists', pediatricians', loan companies - - (not to mention the obstetrician. Ha!)

This new little breed of mother is an all-around lover and a real pal. While dense people scream at her "Hey, are they all yours??" Or would you rather have a number? I have just read the words off of a small slip of paper which fluttered to the floor early one morning as I was packing the six lunches. Out of the packaged box of MilkDuds floated this slip:

"IN CASE OF SHORTAGE OF BOXES PACKED IN CARTON RETURN THIS PACKING SLIP.
(M. J. Holloway)
PACKER NO. 31"

Nothing can be more personal and more comforting when you are all alone and barely able to smile at the bird at six o'clock in the morning. Packer No. 31 apparently really cares if you have the right number of Milk Duds as you are hastily and insanely throwing lunches together while you say your morning prayers:

"Dear Lord, please don't let the children count their Milk Duds, it may lead to an all-day discussion."

At six o'clock in the morning Packer No 31 may be a frumpy, frowzy, sadistically smiling housewife - - just like myself. I gave the bird cage a little shove.

"Who asked him or her to get born anyway?" When you come right down to it even the birds are living unpremeditated existences. No one in the world wants to be merely "a twinkle in their father's eye!"

Everyone has to have their cry-baby days.

While Tom Buck and Patricia Buck are raising their eleven children they get kinda' happy around Income Tax days as we do. Well - - that is until they really start putting down the figures and find out that by the time that the kids get into the beer-drinking age - - they are going to have consumed 76,650 quarts of homogenized milk. Then everyone starts crying. My husband figured with his figures too. He cried:

"Tons and tons of Kotex, shampoo, hair rinse and brassiers! What do they do with those bobby-pins - - eat them? Why can't they wear .88 bras like you do?? And wash their hair with dish detergent like you do?"

Answer: "Children never take after their mothers." At this precise and delicate moment, reality again took the shape of the weekly egg boy who had wandered unwittingly in through the back kitchen door. "Oh, by the way, Darling, do you have $4.00 handy? The egg boy is here with ten dozen eggs. "

The shock was soon and dramatic and he sat there looking like Eddie Albert in Greenacres.

"Ten dozen eggs? Where did he get all those eggs?

I went through the story once more.

"He picks eggs up at an egg farm and they pay him with ten dozen dirty eggs. What is a young boy going to do with ten dozen eggs?

For the first time in our married life we sang together:
"Sell them to someone with a lotta' kids!"
In the togetherness of singing together amidst a torment of tears, I could mentally visualize the voices of the chorus.

Between the eggs and the birdcage my husband said to me: "What are you doing here? Get a job!" So I prayed to the good Lord for courage and I ran up the stairs to the Personnel Office of Texas A&M University and became at-large and at-loose for a day!

She spoke. "Your daughter was in here the other day. She looks just like you around the mouth." I did not know if there was a deeper meaning to her words and I blurted. I need a job." Your typing score is excellent and your test grades were good. I'm sure that the D in Math however can be explained away somehow." On the way to the available Department I kept tripping over my long black skirt with the bright red lines. I decided to try to dramatize my needs today. A lady of leisure lounging in a disheveled pose. No smoking? No sir! The hiring professor took a few looks at me behind the typewriter and spoke. It says here that you have 5 children. ·(I had shrunk my family to half of it's size.) "Now, ah, I've got Ph.D's here to serve and one of your children "mite" get sick or you "mite" get sick." The place was crawling with *mites*.

"How old are you?" he asked.

I did not answer that one.

She said: "You're happy for once that the Feminists got tough. I thought of some really clever adlibs I could have been the proud bearer of. I told them to the children . They loved them.

Dear Old Dad always said: "They sound like they have a hot potato in their mouth!"
Gird up your Loins!
St. Polycarp, Pray for us.

Chapter Nine
"GET A JOB!"

"Heh, heh, heh - so very funny! Especially before my second cup of coffee and an eight o'clock class! Go and find me my Sarte! If you will stop standing around being so Irish and so early, maybe something would get found around here! And where's my belt?"

"It is on Jeanne's neck - - she's a dog this morning."

He said, "Hurry, hurry, hurry - - my belt! My Sarte! It's seven- thirty!!"

"In that case, Sarte is right behind you under the Sears Catalog, and anyway what are you teaching those poor little Aggies?"

He said, "That Irish housewives should be seen and not heard!" He fastened his waistbelt, gave me an Aristotelian kiss, and jumped over the cat who was crying because the con-bird pecked his already sore paw - - hesitated a moment to eye the Texas weather suspiciously and then made a dramatic break for the unknown.

I called after him (I was scared to death to dash

out in my bathrobe) Polly Joe, my neighbor, was always three loads of laundry ahead of me.) "Hey! Wait a minute! What about those ethical theories!" I hoped he wouldn't lose them in the course of the day. He screamed back from the doorway of his Corvette:

"Oh, forget my ethical theories. Most people maintain that Aristotle had one basic ethical theory to work from. I maintain that he had four! Don't forget to pick Jeanne up from kindergarten!"
And I screamed back, "Don't forget the tomatoes and lettuce! Or we won't have any salad to work from!"

He is a good ole ' boy to say the least. A Bohemian indeed, in whom I could find no guile.

I went back into the bedroom to dress. "What can I buy from Sears today that I don't need?" I mused - picking up the Sears Catalog. I was instantly horrified to see Being and Nothingness staring menacingly up at me from the dresser. Horrors. Now what will the professor talk about this morning? Perhaps he can improvise for an hour and a half with talk about weights and measures? I was going to open Being and Nothingness and just dangerously "peek" inside but the last time that

I did that I became so unglued that the children thought that I had lost my eyebrow pencil again. Sartre makes me angrier than Hugh Heffner. About Hugh's Playboy magazine I reason that it is not his fault that a lot of girls have lost their modesty - - as well as their identity.

That evening I was grateful to see the lovable Bohemian return to the family scene of the crime. Some people not only crab about being born, but they come forth with goofy phrases like: "Why was I born black?" or "Why was I born ugly?" or "Why was I born such a sickening white?" or "Why was I born so beautiful?" "Why was I born so dumb?" -- "Born so angry?" "Why was I only born once?" Now that we are here we have that relentless will to live, and not only to live, but somedays -- to love. And crazy as it may seem, even with all of us around torturing him, the old man is still lovable, unbendable, unwrinkable and perma-press.

Like I said - - he came home again and sat on the couch. That crazy, sticky, unlovable couch. He even reclined. He even relaxed. (He did not know that the cat was near with the Texas fleas!) All of a sudden, the charming fellow screamed: "Hey! Where is my left leg?" Everyone has a right to know where their left leg is. Even people who are not philosophers know that this is a right. They have their built-in prenatal wisdom to tell them this.

"Hey! Where is my left leg?" came again the anguished cry from the lovable lad. David said, "It's right here--I'm sitting on it with Maddie and Andrea."

"O.K.," said the amorous Dad, "for a moment I thought I had lost it."

I advocated a suggestion, "Let's communicate. What do you want to talk about?"

The man said, "Oh no you don't! I'm much too tired to fight!"

Me: "Do we have to fight?"

He: "With you Irish, there is no other extreme. Besides being good-looking, you are combative, belligerent, argumentative, ..." (A nine-year old came out from under his right leg, our little daughter Andrea Louise. "Am I Irish?" she pondered.)
And to the dear old reclining Dad I said,

"Well, how did it go in Houston today? How was the lecture by the visiting prof?"

"He was Irish and pugnacious. He had a way of saying personal remarks which really went over in a big way-...but they never really hurt anyone's feelings," he said over his belly.

"Well," I asked, "if he never hurt anyone's feelings with his charming Irish ways--how come he got a bomb in his car and a bullet shot at him?"

"You Irish--you are witty tool" moaned the fellow who by now was staring in stark terror at the cat who had made his appearance by rubbing himself on the back of His neck and had emerged down the side arm of the couch.

I love him. I reached over and pulled the string hanging out of his shirt at the same time thinking what a wonderful couch that it was which could harbour nine people.

As the string returned, the true story of his life came forth:

"Where is the Texaco Touring Atlas?"
"Are your hands sticky?" "Did you go potty?"
"Where is my Wittgenstein?"
"What is that horrible noise?"
"Who stole all my money?"
"Yes. I'll drive you to the store."
"Who is that coming? Miss America?"

An onlooker will see quickly that he is soft on kids, dogs, birds, (Always says: "Are you pickin' on that poor bird again?), calves, Hereford cows, cats, (hates 'em, but is soft on them), armadillos and fish. (Won't catch them).

Every once in a while other housewives-mothers and myself have to blame all of the children's existences on our husbands. On a clear day in the Spokane Valley of the doomed-- you can· hear us scream right through the murmuring pines and the hemlocks:

"They are all his children!"

The echo came back from the dusty halls of the world.

"They are his kids, tooooo And don't forget itttt!"

The way that we cook you would never guess that we think: that our children are his too. We cook like we have a guilty conscience. It looks as though we did have something to do with the unpremeditated existences ourselves as we plow through mounds of dirty clothes and ponder endlessly, "Wonder which soap will get them the cleanest??"

Before an old movie with Susan Hayward there was printed some words by Lillian Roth: "My life was chartered out for me -- even before I was born!" Most of us just came upon the scene of life as did Diana Moon Glampers:

"A mystifying equation that had thrust her into life as pointlessly:

'My mother was a Moon. My father was a Glampers!'" (Kurt Vonnegut, Jr.)

No one planned anything definite for some of us to be and if they would have - - we certainly would have fought it all of the way.

By now it looks clearer that maybe we did have something to do with the unpremeditated existences and one of my friends who is smarter than I am screams on a clearer day:

"I think that I should get some credit tooooo!"

Once again we are dangerously close to that perennial question which comes out of the dust of time, now and then, When you least expect it:

"How many ya' got?" "Are they all yours?"

We ponder the intrinsic meaning of this interrogation: Does this mean?

That: "Are some of them test-tube babies?"
"Is their father dead?"
"Are they all yours, body and soul?"
"Do they belong to the neighbors?"
"Are they begat by many fathers?"
"And one belongs to your sister-in-law?"

Larger sociological surveys are piling up and obstetricians in fact are becoming King of the Road. They are starting to hate themselves and their profession. One obstetrician that I know and the father of six himself (they are all his) - - said to me: "Why do people have so many children, anyway?" And with my built-in prenatal wisdom I answered him: "Cuz! There is nothing else ·co have!" I moaned in the delivery room as I delivered to him my tenth baby (He had said to the nurse: "Get me the scissors!" I screamed, "No!" The baby cooperated.) "It's another darling little daughter, so that makes eight girls." He said surprised. "It's simple," I said, "just put an "a" on the Robert and call her Roberta Suzanne," I comforted the crying doctor. "Hello, Roberta," he cried. A belated Swedish nurse moaned with a Swedish accent, "It's no cookie to have a baby!" (All the Swedish people think of is pastries.)

I tried to think of something intellectual to say- after all you look pretty dumb in a delivery room anyway and then you bring an unpremeditated existence into the world and everyone is mad at you, and they keep making stupid remarks, so I said; "I just read the book The Organization Man while I was having labor pains and I don't think that the business executive has it any easier! And I certainly don't think that the business executive is more creative than the housewife!"

The poor obstetrician left the scene of creation muttering to himself, but I heard him. "I can't understand a word the sociologists are saying these days. They talk way over my head-in fact that's all they do is talk. They never come upon

the scene!"--- mutter, mutter, and his mutterings ceased and he ceased to be there. I comforted myself, "Well, besides being an obstetrician he is also just someone else's old man," said the old-doll Mamma in the hospital--with a sore bottom.
I won't comfort you by telling that dialog was fiction. It certainly was not.

One day while the philosopher was looking (on a clear day) for a clean shirt I asked him: "What ever happened to Pitrim Sorokin?".

"Pitrim is out!" he surprised me with his unusually sudden reply.

He struggled to tie his shoes. "I warned you to buy loafers," I snickered. "I teach at a conservative university and I'm not going to work lookin' like a clown! It's bad enough that you bought me a gold shirt!"

In the meantime, while the philosopher was wondering if this was "dirty-shirt" day and "no-sock" day - - the other real me was getting upset. "I have a soft spot for Pitrim--he said a lot of real soul-like truths. He is down to earth and his sociology books have real things in them with real people and what is really happening. Whatever happened to Pitrim Sorokin?" I asked--getting tiresome, as is my natural talent.

"Surveys are in!! Pitrim is out!! All they want these days is surveys." I said, "Remember the time that I asked the Sociology Chairman what he was going to do with that desk full of surveys and he muttered something about people who ask questions--and he went out and got stoned?"

"Which tie goes with this gold shirt?" he stood puzzled in his shorts from Sears.

"The orange tie with the blue and brown stripes," I lied as is my usually tricky mean deal. He is so dumb-he always wears what I say. Or could it be that he is lovable and trusting? Anyone putting on an orange tie with a blue and brown stripe on a gold shirt with beige socks naively, has got to be lovable.

"Whenever are you going to cultivate that lost vein of tact and diplomacy that I discussed with you one day - - and when are you going to stop sticking knives into real people?", he moaned.

I said, "I thought that anthropologists studied old bones. Shows how dumb I am. Last week I read in the newspaper this advice from a well-known anthropologist: "The time for population correction is not the year 2000. The time is now. The U.S. could do with two different forms of marriage: One would be the individual marriage. Young people could live together without having children and easily dissolve the union if one or the other got bored with it. On the other hand: we have the parental marriage. Herein the couple is allowed to rear children relieving the strains of parenthood by an occasional adultery." -Mary Margaret Mead

I wonder if she ever thought of an occasional murder? She is the same woman who said that marijuana should be made available for sixteen year olds. That is not different from their old fat mama sipping on a cocktail." I was now getting worried because I could see that the philosopher was getting up his Bohemian. "LEAVE OTHER PEOPLE OUT OF MY LIFE!" I know when I have it pretty cool with three free hots and a lumpy flop so I said carefully, "Here are your socks, they are a little bit damp. Why do you have to wear socks, anyway?"

He growled as only a logical Thomist can, "Everybody wears socks! GET A JOB!!"

When all else is said "GET A JOB!" is all he ever says so I became a loose woman and ran away from home. Just for a day. I ran right up to the Personnel Office at Texas A&M and looked the receptionist right in the eye. "Gosh," thought

I. She looks young enough to be my daughter!"
She looked at me: "CAN YOU TYPE?"
"Can I? I can type up a storm." I answered.
"Electrical or manual?" she asked.
"Electric?" I asked. Thinking to myself, boy, now they are ruining everything with their fancy doodads.
"I need to know" she asked, "so that I can get you a typewriter to take your test on."
"Manual." I answered. "I like to work my way through words."

I was sent to the available Department and looked my would-be employer in the eye. His eyes narrowed when he saw me and a frown furrowed forth--he said, "ARE YOU A PEOPLE PERSON?" My smile froze into a beautiful example of Bell's Palsy--1 could neither say "yay" nor "nay" for I knew not whether a people person was good or bad. Paralyzed to answer the question I did answer: "Yes, I am a people person." I said it proudly and patriotically and I remembered that he was a retired Army Major and I felt that he would be proud of me. His narrowed eyes expanded and his frown burrowed deeper. Foiled again!! And all the way home to the children I kept thinking of some cute things I could have said, like: "Sure. I'm a flying purple people eater!" (The children loved it.)

Dear Old Dad always said: "Just ignore it, maybe it will go away!"
Gird up your Loins
St. Polycarp pray for us

Chapter 10
Ladies: The Basis of Leisure

It seems like just yesterday when Richard used to be my little boy. I received my semi-annual letter from him yesterday.

Dear Mom,

We are testing 240 cows for pregnancy, then shipping them East. What is Dad doing?

P.S. The telephone, MacGregor Lake 26-does not work.

Why it seems just like yesterday when he was saying to me:
"Mom? Can Phillip come in and play monopoly?"
"Mom? Ya got any more of that apple pie left?"
"Mom? Can I have a dog?"
"Mom? Where is the string, the paste, glue, scissors, tape, crayons, pencils, pens, rubber bands, etc.?"
"Mom? Please don't take my rags away from me. A fella can't even wear his rags anymore!"

Teenage daughters are now tacking their pants. I warned them if they get any tighter, I'll have to call the doctor to get them out of their pants. "Tighter! Tighter! My pants are not tight enough!" The girls have been shouting for years. The pants that I got the other day from Sears were a bit loose. I was waiting for the sewing machine to sound when I heard the unbelievable words:

"Awww, that's alright. They look a lot like elephant pants!" I shouted, "What's that? What, who and where are elephant pants?" The answer was unbelievable:

"Elephant pants are baggy pants which are usually gray and which have two large pockets on the bum.

There is a kids TV show which starts with a smiling fellow admonishing coyly and pointing:

"I like you as you are. I think you're so terrific!"

He points at the two and a half year old. She says, "Is he really behind in there?"

I was thinking to myself, "He can talk and sing, he is probably sitting high and dry and never had a baby pee on his lap."

I was still getting the straight dope from the kindergarten kids and I was grateful for that:

"Mark Pooska fell outta the tree. He didn't cry though, just got all muddy. But Lance! Everybody loves Lance! Lance comes out and everybody goes after Lance!" I was suspicious again. "What's that Lance got? I don't know," Jeanne said, and apparently she didn't care. I don't know, everybody just loves Lance!" Those dumb kindergarten kids would love anybody.

As I was sitting out my usual hours in the optometrists' office with my six teenager--there were at the same time- two friends of hers were sitting there. One of the girls was reading Walden. I meditated on how adorable and intellectual and good that she looked. She spoke then to her friend:

"Oh--ye gads! This goes on and on! Six pages on how to make bread! I mean--bread!? Who needs it? Who really cares??"

My good friend, a thirty four year old housewife, who now has eleven children, lives in a very fertile valley of Spokane, Washington. Here, amidst tons and tons of stones and sand--people are able to grow the most fabulous cabbages, beans, cherries, tomatoes, strawberries, peaches, cantaloupes, etc. Lynn Bertis is always busy picking, canning, freezing, and running and jumping.

Jumping over kids, cats, toys, etc., and running on her errands. Baking bread is her specialty. The

Morning Glory Flour Mills Company located not too far from here in the Big Sky country of Montana had the opportunity to taste her bread one day.

"Mrs. Bertis! Where did you get this marvelous bread? And baked with our very own marvelous flour? Oh, Mrs. Bertis, we are so busy packing this flour and making out bills-- could you please bring us six loaves every week for our meals and our lunches?"

Needless to say, Lynn and her husband got a big kick out of that and the common ordinary everyday housewife did not look so ordinary anymore. Lynn chuckled and grinned in her Irish sort of way and she knew the truth that lay swelled up in her heart within, which is as big as the Emerald Isle itself.

George Bernard Shaw said it as only he could: "Gin and Chicken, --lie helpless in her Irish hand."
"You did it! You did it!" sang the flour company with their hair all full of wheat seeds.

Lynn wouldn't even tell Thoreau what she put into that bread dough. One day while I was there and stuffing my mouth full of her homemade peppers Italian style, I heard her humming sadistically to herself.

"Hummmm ta da ta da, A little pound of this and

a half a pound of that."

I screamed, "MOTHER'S OATS???!!!!"

"Shhh, not so loud!" She threatened me with the meat cleaver as only an Irish heart can.

"Stop shouting and I promise to tell you the secret of putting 1/2 of a cup of oats in the wheat bread and all of the reasons for and against."

"Horrors! You could write a thesis with that information!" I was getting hysterical. "You could write a thesis, that is, if you did not babysit for half of the neighborhood, play the organ at Mass, write music for songs, give piano lessons to anyone who walks in the house and put on church variety shows! Lynn whispered, "I don't want to appear rude, but if you have finished with your eating maybe you can help me catch the pig. It got out today and it might bite one of the babies. After that, we will pick beans and then chop fifty pounds of rhubarb. After that...."

I remember the day, of course, that I met Lynn. I was still suffering then from the traumatic shock of moving. Call it movers-trauma. I stared at the unvarnished floors, up at the high ceilings of the house, I gawked. Then a mysterious knock came at the tall overbearing door. Who did I know? "Probably just the Lutheran Minister and his wife--only this and nothing more." In Alabama, the Lutherans were the first people to discover us. Just then a voice from the slowly opened door. "Hi! I'm your close neighbor. I'm in rather a hurry, I just brought an old lady's laundry back to her.

The voice grabbed up one of our 1000 crayons and wrote her phone number large on a piece of paper. "Here you are, if you ever need a friend- here is my phone number." The voice started to leave. "Who are you and where did you come from?" I gasped.

"Just your nutty neighbor, see you!" She was off in a cloud of dust in her old red pick-up truck with kids screaming and hanging off of the sides. I didn't trust her, she looked too real.

And after we chop the rhubarb we will be the first ones to pick a flat of strawberries. Of course, we shall have to take seventeen children with us..... and then after that."

I took off myself in a cloud of the valley dust. I feel very insecure to be constantly surrounded by humanity. I don't mind ten or twelve kids some of the time, but when Lynn invites one child, the child invariably says, "but I have four brothers and three sisters." "Bring 'em along!" says Lynn enthusiastically—"We'll bring three cars instead of two!"

One day, when we lived in Texas, I went over to visit with Mary's fifth grade teacher. "I got your note about coming to see Mary's SRA results---how is my Mary doing?" I smiled at her teacher. She was very young and very pregnant. One day Mary told me, "I think my teacher is going to have a baby someday, Mom, she has one of those, you know, kind of fat dresses." The fourteenager, Irene, overheard her: "Only eleven years old! What does she know about people having babies?"

I am not worried about Mary--she wants to be rich when she grows up. I am worried about her teacher. Every child in her class had their turn to go out with the measles. That is not the worst of the story, however. She told me that when her baby is born, her mother and her mother-in-law are both coming down to help her out. And then she said, "THEN I'M GOING TO BE A LADY OF LEISURE!" My tongue dried up. I wanted so badly to tell her of the hazards of becoming a do-it-yourself mother and an all-by-yourself housewife. It had developed in upper Canada many times that women---when they became isolated housewives, get jumpy.

Clara Boothe Luce doesn't help the situation any, either, when she says: "Today's young husband subconsciously or consciously knows that in the restaurant down the street there is a very pretty waitress!" What does that mean? What is logical to follow from that premise? Does it follow that then the big fat mama at home cannot cook a mean sausage? Or does it follow from that, that the big, fat mama at home cannot kiss? (Syllogism, anyone?)

One day I am frying bacon and the Philosopher King wanted a kiss. "Careful!" I warned him.
"The children have eyes!" He whispered again.
"Careful!" I warned. "The children have ears!" And after I got the bacon burned I contemplated:

"Why in the world would anyone want to contemplate on nothingness?"
"Well, my dear," said the Philosopher putting salve on his bacon burns, "you are just not very metaphysical. In actual fact--you are A CONSUMER! All that women think about is becoming more and more! That is all that women are capable of; women never think about coming nothing." (Becoming more and more??? Is this why they are always pregnant?!!!)

"Well", I said, do you remember the time that I

was screaming that I was becoming smaller and smaller?"

He said, "But remember your friend in Alabama who was screaming that she was getting bigger and bigger." I said that I thought it was bad for her to be milking that cow morning and night. "Well," I said, "I still think that it is a waste of time contemplating nothingness. When we die we still have our deadness and our souls. Now it was the philosopher's turn to be hysterical. "Our deadness! What in the world is that?"

Ha! Perhaps I stumped a Thomistic philosopher. Ha! I have to clean the birdcage now. He or she ate another bread wrapper.

"Yes, there is a good girl", he admonished. "You clean the birdcage and contemplate your deadness."

I cleaned the birdcage while shrieks of hysterical laughter percolated from the bathroom.

"And I lie there with my deadness
And my soul went marching on
To better worlds."

Ladies: Suppose now that you are in the A&P picking out rotten bananas and then someone shouts:

"Why, after all, should there be such a thing as a banana? Why not just NOTHING?"

Here is a quote by Josef Pieper from Leisure, The Basis of Culture:

"But all the same, just try to imagine that all of a sudden, among the myriad voices in the factories, and in the open market square, "Where can we get this, --that or the other?" That all of a sudden among those familiar voices and questions another voice was to be raised:

Asking "Why, after all--should there be such a thing as being. Why not just nothing?" This is the age old philosophical cry of wonder that Heidegger called the basic metaphysical question.

To St. Thomas it would be utterly ridiculous for man to undertake to defend the Cuestion. Creation needs no justification. Here we are back, imagining again that we are in the A&P----picking through the rotten bananas. And someone is shouting:
"Why--after all--should there be such a thing as bananas? Why not just NOTHING?" And the Thomistic Philosopher wanted more than being and

nothingness and he shouted through the bananas- "GET A JOB!"

I was a loose woman quickly. All eyes stared upon me as I bounded into the Personnel Office at Texas A&M (all out of breath from the hike up the stairway). "I need a job", I said. "Can you type?" Came the answer. "You have my application," I said weakly.

As I walked into the available Department opening, I put my best face on. It was my "Lucy" face (no, not St. Lucy!). It was a face that showed love for the world and any possible obstacle. The man with the mad face said to me: "Do you have any babies who will wake you up during the night and then you won't want to come to work the next day?" I looked around and saw one with a pregnant belly and knew of several more. Instead of answering the mad man "yay" or "nay" as the Bible says, I say, "There are a lot of girls working here who are pregnant and who have babies in the nurseries."

The mad face got madder and I was given a dishonorable discharge before I could even cry. On the way home to the children I thought of all the funny things I could have said and missed the chance (the children loved them).

Dear Old Dad always said, "You can't please all of the people all of the time. Only some of the people some of the time."
Gird up your Loins
St. Polycarp, Pray for us

Chapter Eleven
Split Ends

This is the only right chapter title for a book with eight daughters. Split Ends. I thought maybe the split ends would end when the third oldest daughter left home. Leave them alone and they'll come home--dragging their ends behind them.

It caught onto "the next batch". Now I still hear: "Look, Mom. How many split ends do you see"?

Forty-five years since then, my 19 year old granddaughter, Leah Christine, who had long hair, said to me, "Grandma, I just cut 7 inches off my hair". I looked at her suspiciously. "SPLIT ENDS?" "Yes" she said. I wouldn't know a split end from a right end tackle. The most I ever heard about hair was when Dear Old Dad used to tell me, "It looks like the cat got her hair!"

Our eleven year old daughter said: "What's this next batch Mom?" I explained to her how near ages went through more life together. She is the "next batch" along with her sisters Roberta and Madeline. We try to say the three names all together as fast as we can when we want to say: "who" is going? Or "who" is coming? Or "who" is staying? We say it fast and it sounds like one person is going, coming, or staying.

"Bobby-Maddie-Jeanne-Dick-Rick-Dave!"

There lies no vile intention to crush the spirit or the individual personality. They all sleep in a separate bed and they all have different ideas. "What one doesn't think of, the other one will" is a famous American dialogue. This proves their individuality. When I was a child the cry was: "She has a mind of her own! Agghhh!! Look out for her!" In the 1930's they resented it.

A last chapter that is written two years after the other chapters cannot hope to mirror the preceding style but it provides a lot of insight into lives unfolding.

Things haven't changed too much in two to five years. Irene, who was 14 five chapters ago, is now 19 and "whoop-te-doing" it because Oona and John are back together again. David was a talkative 12 six chapters ago, and is now a talkative 18. He has conned the mind right out of his own father. He asked his father if he would be more quiet so that he wouldn't wake him up every morning. "Every morning all I hear is Dad." It's pretty rough when you've been at a beer party to listen to people getting ready for school and for work. He doesn't con me though!! I just have the habit of lending my car to 18 yr. olds who bring it back stinking of beer and covered with mud. The very first night he borrowed the family Ford wagon the whole A-Frame fell off. "I was just driving along when all of a sudden the wheel came off!" quoted Dave. There was a different story from Thatcher's Midway Transmission Shop. "Wow!! You had to drive into a heck of a hole to knock that A-Frame off, Mrs. Becka!"

At the beginning of this book people felt as though they had to leave home to find themselves. Remember the PHD's in the kitchen? Well the feeling in 1974 is still floating around. A 37-yr old mother left home which consisted of:

1. A 12-room house
2. Her own car
3. Expensive clothes
4. Security
5. Her career as an art history professor
6. The approval of society
7. A husband and a 12 yr. old daughter in Emporia, Kansas

She left all this to find herself and instead she found a lot of other women who left their homes to find themselves and they all found each other. Now they have each other for company. "I don't think I'm any different from other women. We're all time bombs" she said. She claimed that the physical distance between them promotes mutual respect and improves communication. Another woman, a member of the Canadian Parliament claimed that very truth also. She had said. "A marriage and a career can be carried on at one time---on the telephone!"

But this woman's claim is that she was raised "in a small Texas town, where she was programmed, first by her parents---and then by her peers--to become wife and mother". If she had not gone off to find herself "I would have hated him (her husband) if I had stayed another year," she says of John, from whom she is now divorced. He's definitely still a part of my family and we all spend Christmas together every year. I refuse to take part any more in institutions that oppress- marriage, motherhood as practiced in Emporia, Kansas, the Episcopal Church, and political parties." (Sunday Eagle, Aug. 4, 1974)

I never did find out if she found herself. She found all those other women and found clearer communications on the telephone too.

There is a famous quote hanging over at A&M

in about every third Department that provides one with a frustrating psychology:

I know you think you understand What you heard me say
But I'm not sure you understand that What you thought you heard May not have been exactly what I meant." (Author Misunderstood)

Does not that want one to grind one's teeth?

It matches up side by side with Dear Old Dad's psychology. I refuse to call it Philosophy because that dear word is always misinterpreted. There are people in this world who change their socks and their underwear every day and maintain: "And that is my Philosophy of Life"! Philosophy is something else. Philosophers don't mean to pull the wool over your eyes, neither do the Scientists. It doesn't matter if Philosophy and Science are over some people's heads----the basics are not for everyone. Philosophy, just like Science, is necessary to keep the World on an even social and spiritual plane. "Who are you?" "Where did you come from?" "Where are you going?" It's no laughing matter.

I know you think you understand what you heard me say.

Unless you become as little children, you'll never be able to fit into the high chair again. And you will never enter the Kingdom of Heaven!

Ya' gotta hand it to Erma Bombeck. She always hits the nail on the head and nary a twain shall meet. Her article on the reasons why people should convert to a one-kid family was superb. The reasons why people should convert to a one-kid family is to completely obliterate SIBLING RIVALRY!! No more Wars With The Ketchup!! She says. I know a one-kid family one time and the little boy was jealous of their mother's affection for the father.

An ex-school teacher friend read this book and said that she liked it better than The Love Machine. I don't know what kind of machine she compared it to, but I did find out later that the woman who wrote the book never went to college and her husband was a TV Producer. That may be an influence to get a book published, maybe not. But with a philosopher for a husband, what earthly chance is there? A Thomist? Who can stand it? Or bear the burden? If A&M ever finds out what a Thomist is, he'll get called in for going incognito. Rightnow they think a Thomist may be "something or someone in Physics".

A woman who works at A&M (no doubt her husband is a professor there too!) got visibly angry when she found out they had a Philosophy Department there. "Why!! I didn't know they had that here!! I thought it was just Agricultural and Mechanical". That mechanical feeling is what they like. It makes everyone feel programmed. I reassured her that it would be kept down to a college roar-with only 6 professors in the Philosophy--(in 1968) compared to 60 professors in Chemistry.

At A&M what really makes news is when Skip Walker gets into one of the classes. Now you are in the Who's Who area.

Sixty years ago, A&M was just a favorite football team coming over the wireless on Scranton Road in Cleveland, Ohio to us. Here we are living the reality. This year they are winning again. 1974. Texas Tech came here to Bryan, College Station last Saturday. My husband, being one of the lower paid professors, watched the game in the MSC building in the TV room with a family of three children and a woman my age. (Her husband probably being another lower paid professor). To his amazement, she stood up at half time and shouted for them to get that lousy show band of Texas Tech off of the field---screaming for her Fightin' Aggie Band. The band of military precision. She was enraptured when they came on and she stood the entire time as though they were the national anthem themselves. All of this corner of Texas is fightin' Aggie mad!

When they beat Tech, it made front page headlines in the Sunday Eagle. The sports editor made the headlines.

RED-HOT AGGIES WRECK RAIDERS
"The Texas Aggies, at first merely sparring with the visiting Southwest Conference co-leader Texas Tech, used some wicked right-handed punches, namely Skip Walker, to leave he Red Riders tired, bewildered, and confused by halftime..."

The inside headlines read: "A&M Destroys Ninth Ranked Tech."

Yes, football is a very violent affair. They all got a new car too. And wear armor just like the gladiators of old. I was glad that I went to that party where the Aggie Astronomer told me the story of how A&M got their Philosophy Department.

One fine day, a past President of A&M was interviewed by Time magazine. There followed an issue of Time where he was interviewed was as such "Do you have a Philosophy Department in your University?" "No", said the obedient Military man. When he saw his dialogue in print, he immediately called in his Vice President and ordered Army style: "Whatever that Department is!! I WANT ONE!!"

I saved a postcard we got from our other son. He is not as talkative as David and Madeline.

"Dad,
Got your check. Thanks for the advice.
Rick."

It's fun following people around that use food stamps. I had imprinted on my memory a huge poster which hung on the wall of the food stamp office. Therewas the picture of a house bursting its natural seams and rocking on its foundation. (??) Underneath the house was the citation:

"Is your house bulging at the seams? Perhaps there are too many folks inside already!" The advice follows to contact the Family Planning Unit on the next block.

I wrote a letter to the Editor about it and the poster disappeared after three years of intimidation. Now there is a poster with a cute, fat, pregnant little lady with acaption under her which says: "Free formula for your new baby!" Another cute, fat, pregnant, little lady also says: "Free milk for you!!" The Family Planning RN wrote me a long letter about how only planned babies can be wanted babies and only planned-wanted babies can be loved babies.

She told me all about her **and her** daughter who her whole life revolved around and who was the essence of her own life.

Dick has a book on the he Battered Baby Syndrome. The statistics in it for the high-percentage of battered babies are the planned-wanted babies. Whatever happened to Pitrim Sorokin??

My sweet and industrious friend has been the sole support of her children ever since her husband passed away years ago. She has acquired a MA in her Middle Age and is now earning a believable salary as the English and Spanish teacher of the 8th and 9th grades in a junior high school. When she made out her application, she pointed out to me that you have to be careful what you say. If they find out that you have eleven children, they will come to the conclusion that you do not have enough sense, therefore, to teach school.

This is the reason for "can you remember all of their names"? This question implies mental deficiency. However, there was a place on the application for No. of Children. (They like to know that because it enhances their lives). On that blank she put: "2 dependent children." On the next blank: "No. of people living at home blank she put 4 children and herself. This got one lady very mixed up and taken up so she took the application to a higher up. "What does this mean? The lady clamored to know.

"It means just what it says" said the higher-up who knew Virginia and who knew that she had eleven children. "She has 2 children that are dependent on her and the other two that are living at home and are not dependent on her." It was as plain as mud.

----BACK AT THE RANCH!!!----

Every single morning when I come down totally unprepared for the disaster of the day. The Good Lord helped me when he told me to "be not solicitous for the morrow---sufficient for the day are the notes you find on your desk in the morning, thereof." My eyes are half shut but I can discern the scribble:

"Mom:

Don't use the car. Tribbey said a throwout bearing costs about $8.00. If you can get Dad to buy it, then Tribbey said he would help me put it in. If you drive the car anymore it will go out and then you will need a new clutch and pressure plate which costs a lot more.
David."

I opened the garage door and stared tiredly at the old lawn mower which was being "repaired" by David. And it stopped short, never to go again-

---I thought of my left and right turn signal, also repaired by David, which now blows the horn instead. I thought of the Good Lord.

Dear Old Dad always said: "Put up or shut up!" He would say to me with a stern stare. Oddly enough it gave me additional meditation material.

"Put up or shut up!"

He was trying to tell me something. "Put up or shut up!" And "never put all your eggs into one basket!" He cautioned to me as he sidled out of the door to work. I pondered the heavy words of God-Wisdom---errrr People Wisdom (That's not in Scripture!). At the age of eight I pictured myself putting all the eggs that I had into one basket--hey!! I had too many eggs and I couldn't get them all into one basket!! They threatened to fall!!

Mother can hardly bear the whiney bearing-down tone of Bob Dylan and Father cannot bear it at all. Mothers can shut out sounds easier than Dads can.

Mothers can operate when children are playing house and school under their very own feet. LOVE, as such, always comes to Mother's support whenever she comes across little notes that her little daughters write to one another while playing house:

"To Bobby,

Will you be my little girl and then be my little boy and then be my dog---ummmm and then I will be your little girl and your little boy and then your dog.

Love, Madeline

P.S.
Write Yes __ Write No__

These days it is sort of equivalent to having the Bubonic Plague having a larger family. Day to day you get counted. Smile God Loves You. Keep smiling, the Boss loves idiots. People don't smile at you anymore and the local priest doesn't say "have more babies!!" They don't smile anymore. Grimace!! The largest house you can afford to buy is a 3-bedroom because that is the most they build!!

It sort of reminds me of a story a friend of mine told me. She is in her 50's now and I'm in my 40's but we still remember the roaring 20's. One day her mother and father were at work (this was in Missouri!) she came across, quite accidentally (as all children come across things), an old letter written to her mother from her mother's sister. The letter said:

"Grace, why didn't you tell me about this baby?? You did not tell me a word about this child!"
From this bit of hasty information, Virginia came to the conclusion as follows: "No wonder my parents don't like me! "I'm not been their child!!"

We got all kinds of subconscious ideas from our environment. That's sure!! I was standing next to a lady in front of Cook's Department store one day, meditating on the Christian display. We were looking now at Nativity scenes. She said: "it looks like their Nativity scenes are only $2.99. I've been thinking about getting one-- and then she walked away hastily and shouted back at me- "IF I DONT GET IN THE WRONG PEW AND GET BUSTED!!."

I received a note from the children:

"Dear Parents,

Our school will join the many other schools in Bryan that will make a box available where students may put their left over candy from Halloween. The candy will be collected and sent to retarded children in Austin State school. On CHRISTMAS EVE the candy will go to over 1,000 children who remain

Are They All Yours?

in the Austin dorms during the holiday season." Now I think I'll believe any rumors about schools. My husband just had seven of the children's teeth cleaned. And it was "Dad! No Cavities!!" all down the line.

But let us meditate on the big things that really complicate the lives of parents. Today I had to buy some plastic straws at the "Safeway for the 6th grader's art class. I was standing in front of the straws and then I didn't know whether to buy the plastic straws or the paper straws. Whether to buy the straws that bend or the straight straws. They needed the straws that day so I made my purchases and went out of the Safeway muttering to myself:
"Plastic or paper? Straight or bending?"

"Goody! Goody! She bought the good ones!!" was the far out cry as they clutched the bending plastic straws from my hands. I drove away rust and all. David was with me. "Mom, did you see that big fat man who walked into the Safeway when you came out??" he said.

"Was I supposed to?" I said starting the car. "Well, he had a big sheet of paper stuck to the back of his pants. David never misses a thing! Except his lunch because he sleeps too long---and procuring a job where he can mind his own business!!!!

It is the BIG things in life that complicate the lives of parents!! Especially at 7 o'clock in the morning: "Mom!! Did you get the medicine for my blackheads?? Not the ONE that KEEPS THEM FROM COMING!! The ONE that TAKES THEM AWAY!!"

Aghhhhhhhhhhhh!!

When a friend of mine, a professional musician, saw the title to this pseudo book she said, "When people ask me "Are They All Yours?" I have now learned to answer: "No!! Four of them are mine and four of them are HIS!!"

Now the really BIG COMPLEXITIES OF LIFE I try to shirk. On our vacation last summer, my husband of twenty-six years treated me to a breakfast from a scenic window in a restaurant in Colville, Washington. I felt like a bride on her honeymoon. I didn't give second thoughts about the five children and the dog back at the Motel eating sugared corn pops in front of a TV. I studied the menu like a freshman at college.

"EGGS, ANY STYLE". Hit my fancy and my funny bone. My husband spoke out very seriously, I'm going to have eggs over easy, what are you going to have?" "St. John of the Cross couldn't have been more proud of me at that moment. I obliged: And said: "I'll take---EGGS, ANY STYLE. Surprise me!"

Truly, the Bohemian in which I have found no guile---said "Stop that!" Now here was a man who had to have questions and answers according to right reason! St. Thomas said: When one's anger is in accordance with right reason, one's anger is deserving of Praise!"

The Pride in my Detachment and the pride in my morbid sense of humor turned into a fear of loss of identity. I cried through my clandestine tears:

"EGGS! Make mine SUNNYSIDE UP!"

Dear Old Dad always said: "All in together boys! Never mind the weather boys!"
Gird up your Loins!
St. Polycarp, Pray for us!

Chapter Twelve
A McDonald Catharsis (Rich vs Poor)

No one wants to feel guilty for anything, especially for bringing children into the world. Dear Old Dad always looked guilty for bringing me into the world but always insisted: "There is always room for one more!" Wouldn't it be wonderful if everyone said that!   He also said, "There is no such word as can't!" He never used the word **"can't"**. His word was "Do" read a good book. "Ladies do not cross their legs!" (He did not say can't).

Mrs. Obama complains about all the fat children! We can humbly say that we never had any fat kids. Now that our children have left home and we still have a home left, we, and other older people, use McDonalds for a morning breakfast and a Catharsis of our ills.

One man who never had children used to complain about his wife's plants. "Those darn plants! I hate them!" he moaned.

Another man whose wife was overweight could not get a job at A&M. I told my husband that A&M students had a bumper sticker that read, "No Fat

Chicks!" He denied it.

Another man moaned, "If I knew that I was going to live this long, I would have taken better care of my teeth!"

One lady said, "When I had to quit smoking, I was just my old boring self!"

A man came up to my husband and told him that he didn't just get things out of books; he was a real philosopher.

One wealthy lady saw me standing every morning while my husband ordered our breakfast. She walked up to me to say, "Irene, do you have 10 dollars I can borrow? I left my money at home. Quickly, without thinking, I said, "No, I'm not allowed." Her face got that "woman hate man" look. I added, "If I had any money, I would give it to my children." "That's true" she said, and walked away satisfied.

Everyone seemed to know who the rich and poor were at McDonald's. I knew a wealthy lady sitting at a table, she said "hello" to me. A wealthy lady standing there said to her, "You don't know her!" "Yes I do", said the sitting lady, "she comes in church all the time!" (Was I allowed?)

While at McDonalds we ran into a man from our church. He said to me, "I'm poor! And you are poor!" People really take notice of who is who! Everyone notices if you have a new car or an old car. Sometimes you can fool them. You can be rich and drive an old car!

As I stood there with my friend, a man came by to ask him if he would show him how to set up for a funeral. He replied, "No, I won't help." The man's face fell. "I went to the Pediatric Hospital! My heart!" My friend said. "What's wrong with your heart?" I wondered. "TOO MUCH LOVE!!" he said. To the other man he said, "I will help you set up for the funeral!!"

I started to think, Rich-poor, Rich-poor, Drunk-sober, Drunk-sober. Everyone can go into church! A man used to come into church so drunk you could smell him a few feet away. He would bring in his mother to buy her a rosary and a lady stuck closely by him to hear him say, "Do you want a rosary too, Mary?" Two rosaries were picked out as he picked a wad of bills out of his pocket. The salesclerk had shouted, "Here comes my best customer!" The scene always repeated itself. I said to him, "Why don't you study in Austin to be a Deacon?" I thought the experience might sober him up or we could use a drunk deacon if he did not preach heresy. I told two students it doesn't matter if you come to church drunk or sober, rich or poor, as long as you come. They nodded knowingly.

Someone put a large sign outside of church.
"PREGNANT? NEED HELP?" It should have read, "DRUNK? NEED HELP?"
A lady's Catharsis over her pancakes at Mickey D's was this, "Why do I have to suffer?"

My husband's Catharsis at McDonalds was the loudest!! "I dragged my children all over the United States and Canada!!" I told this to our daughter, Mary Elizabeth, and she said, "But we were happy."

A documentary of Humanly Unpremeditated Existences refers to Jeremiah the Prophet. Read Jeremiah Chapter 1:4-5. "The word of the LORD came to me, saying, "Before I formed thee in the bowels of thy Mother, I knew thee, and before thou comest forth out of the womb, I sanctified thee, and made thee a prophet unto the nations."

The Bible does not say that his mother and his father had any clue Jeremiah was destined by God to be a prophet.

It is dangerous physically to be a prophet. Isaiah was sawed in half and Jeremiah was stoned to death by his countrymen for threatening them with the punishment of God.

There is a Sheriff in Arizona who people would like to kill because he is trying to keep the law. He is trying to protect the border between Mexico and Arizona. People in the USA prefer CHAOS. They tried to get all of the Catholics out of Mexico, and now they are trying to force them back in.

A voice for Peace was silenced on March 16, 2002 when the Archbishop of Cali Columbia, Isaiah Duarte Cancina, was shot several times in the head and chest at point blank range by gunmen who were waiting for him outside of a church after he had witnessed the marriage vows of 100 couples in a group ceremony. The killers escaped on a motorcycle. Archbishop Isaiah had been an outspoken critic of guerrilla violence and drug trafficking. Isaiah's parents never knew their son would be a martyr for believing in God. At a large church meeting, they asked us:

"What do we have that NO ONE ELSE HAS?" A lone lady raised her hand and answered: "OUR NAME!" The priest said she was right!! She also could have said: "OUR VOICE!"

My sister-in-law could not have children for 6 years. She wanted to adopt but her husband said:

Only ONE. The adoption agency liked her so much that she finally had 7 children. One child was deaf and went to college. Another child preferred to go to jail. When one boy got a job and bought a new car, he said to his Dad, "Dad, why don't you ever buy a new car?"

"Did you see that water tower over there? I filled it up 1,000 times with cereal, milk, vegetables, etc." his dad said. The child had no clue that the food he ate cost money.

Two nurse friends came over one day and seated themselves on two hard backed chairs, presumably to check out the show. After they had studiously monitored everyone, one little girl about 10 years came up to them and seriously said, "I'm number 7!" They said, "You're number 7!!" they repeated seriously. Apparently Andrea had an insight into their reason for coming. The Professor sat across the room reading his book and did not give a glance.

Still in a serious mood and obviously thinking, "We observed what we came her to observe." They then said, "Well, we'd better go" and they left as seriously as they came.

They didn't go to Mickey D's, they went to a Supermarket that hands out free Cokes and snacks and that is their lunch! Ha! That is how rich people live. Howard Delaney had a class at Loyola in California called, "Philosophy of Laughter." It's hard to make some people laugh. Even St. Laurence couldn't make people laugh when they were frying him on a gridiron and he said: "Turn me over, I'm done on that side".

The McDonald Catharsis is not limited to our favorite McDonalds. It is the same for morning older people everywhere that there is a Mickey D's. My Texan neighbor next door told me that she went to the bank and the lines were so long and tiring. I said, "I'll bet the lines at the churches aren't long and tiring". Margie laughed so hard-- and when Margie Williams laughs it seems like the heavens have opened and God is laughing too.

One mama complained that when a person died and had gotten to 300-400 lbs., it was difficult to squeeze him into the coffin on all sides! That is a reasonable morning complaint! Another lady who was a lawyer said: "I hated my parents, but I loved school." A very unusual remark.

What it all boils down to is that everyone really wants to become a SAINT! That is a built-in desire! It's the bottom line!

St. Polycarp, who had been a disciple of St.

John the Evangelist, was arrested. The Magistrate pressed him to repent and to revile Christ. His reply was: "No." The Procounsel said: "I have wild beasts! I will throw thee to them!" Polycarp said: "Call them. Repentance from better to worse is a change we cannot make."

One Philosophy Professor said, "I could try 265 different ways and I would never make it!" St. Catherine of Sienna watched the Seminarians coming down the staircase outside of her window she said: Why should Jesus Christ get all the bandy-legged ones?"

Flannery O'Connor had the best solution said, "I could never be a Saint, but I could be a martyr if someone killed me real quick!" I asked my Priest one day if the people who are Beautified in heaven? He said, "Yes." Then I said, "Why do they have to be canonized?"

He shouted as he escaped into his office, "For the Edification of the People!!" My husband said, "Did you set a trap for him?"

One day Bobbie Sue, age 10, and I helped Mrs. Griffin who belongs to that desirable group called, The Daughters of the American Revolution. We helped her to take a bath as she was ill. As we were getting her out of the tub, we received a phone call telling us to hurry to the hospital because Mary Elizabeth was going to have a baby.

When we got to the hospital we found out that Mary had brought her sister Andrea Louise her lunch and Dr. Lindsay saw her and had her checked out and told her to stay. She was going into labor.

While we were standing there the Sister in charge of admissions called us over and said, bluntly, "Where is Mary's money for her baby?

I called Dad up on Sister's phone. He said, "Mary's money is right here. It's all saved up. But don't tell Sister!!"

All of a sudden Bobbie Sue started dramatically swinging her arms around and said to the nun, "You see, Sister, it is this way. Mary didn't know she was going to have a baby and Dr. Lindsay told her she was going to have a baby!!"

The determined nun could not take it anymore and tried to conceal a reluctant smile. If she ever went to McDonalds in the morning she would have a lot of Catharsis to unlead.

There are more important things to be concerned

about now that it is 2013.
1. Climate changes in Bangladesh.
2. Can videos teach our children Social Skills?
3. More trouble brewing over Temple Mount.
4. Where is the Ark of the Covenant?

    Dear Old Dad always said, "When I die I want to be able to say I've done my share of suffering in this world."
    He gave his heart to Jesus Christ.
Gird up your Loins of Understanding!
St. Polycarp, Pray for us!

Epilogue

Dear Old Dad always said: "All work and no play makes Jack a dull boy." What makes us dull? We use too many idle words.

"But I tell you that every idle word man speaks, they will give an account for it in the Day of Judgement," Matthew Chapter 12:36-37. It was said before in Isaiah, Chapter 58, "and to speak that which profiteth not!"

Every time I said this to my husband, he shuddered. It was very traumatic for him. He said he never wrote a book "because there were TOO MANY WORDS IN THE WORLD ALREADY!" "If you do write a book, please don't use those big words!" I begged.

Everyone at Mickey D's would agree with me, especially in the morning. They were all mad at him already for being an unregenerate Thomist, who couldn't stand to hear animals talk! They wanted to kill him but they were too busy drinking their coffee. They envisioned he was going to create a new McDonalds sandwich-----a McThomist!

Dear Old Dad always said, "Everybody wants to

get into the act!"
Gird up your Loins
St. Polycarp, Pray for us!
The Pregnant End from the Beginning.

AFTERWARD

Mother's Day
Everybody's story starts with a Mother. Thank you for giving my life a happy start.

I had a peaceful Mother's Day. I spent time with all of my children, and my granddaughter, Elizabeth. Babies are so sweet.

Love,
Ann

Madeline sent a card that said:

Because of you, Mom, I know what family is.
It's laughing, it's being real, and being friends.

I love you!
Madeline

Happy Birthday, Mom
Nov. 11, 2014

It always amazes me that if it wasn't for you, many of us would not be here.

Your sacrifices have not gone unnoticed. Thank you for showing me how to love and receive love thru your unselfishness.

Thank you for raising me to love God who gives me strength and helps me to be a good person. I am grateful to have a Mother who loved me enough to want God in my life.

I love my life and children, siblings, nieces, and nephews.

Love,
Jeanne-Marie

By the Author:

A prominent priest said there are two kinds of time. One corporal time and one spiritual. Measured by Corporal time, one is 80 years of age, an old woman or man. Measured by spiritual time, his or her soul may remain very young. My greatest happiness is to hear my grandchildren say, "Grandma". My 7-year old granddaughter, Danielle Brooke, said, "When I get big, will I be a great granddaughter?"

Born on November 11, 1928, in Liverpool, England, I came to the USA with Dear Old Dad on the Cunard Liner S.S. Laconia. A Dr. and his wife on the ship wanted to adopt me. Dear Old Dad asked, "Are you Catholic"? They replied, "No". Then Dad said, "No!" That was from the training of the Jesuits in Sacred Heart Parish Liverpool.

Recently I had a breath of fresh air when our oldest daughter, who had been through the more difficult times of our lives, sent me this note:

"Thank you for being my mom
For caring all these years and doing your best.
For always being there when we got home.
For not giving up on us."
Signed, Ann

My "Mum" died when I was born, so I cannot blame her for anything! My faults and transgressions are my own! I can only say:

"Mia Culpa! Mia Culpa! Mia Maximus Culpa !!!"

Amen!

CPSIA information can be obtained
at www.ICGtesting.com
Printed in the USA
BVOW11s1813230417
482042BV00015B/344/P